ENTERING TERESA OF AVILA'S
INTERIOR CASTLE

Entering
Teresa of Avila's
Interior Castle

A Reader's Companion

GILLIAN T. W. AHLGREN

Paulist Press
New York/Mahwah, N.J.

Excerpts from *Teresa of Avila: The Interior Castle,* from the Classics of Western Spirituality, translated by Kieran Kavanaugh, OCD, and Otilio Rodriguez, OCD. Introduction by Kieran Kavanaugh, OCD. Preface by Raimundo Panikkar. Copyright © 1979 by the Washington Province of Discalced Carmelites, Inc. Pubished by Paulist Press, Inc., New York/Mahwah, N.J. Used with permission of Paulist Press.
www.paulistpress.com

Cover design by Trudi Gershenov
Book design by The HK Scriptorium, Inc.

Library of Congress Cataloging-in-Publication Data

Ahlgren, Gillian T. W., 1964–
    Entering Teresa of Avila's *Interior castle* : a reader's companion / Gillian T. W. Ahlgren.
        p. cm.
    Includes bibliographical references.
    ISBN 0-8091-4316-X (alk. paper)
    1. Teresa, of Avila, Saint, 1515–1582. Moradas. 2. Spirituality—Catholic Church. 3. Mysticism. 4. Catholic Church—Doctrines. I. Title.
    BX2179.T4M7263 2005
    248.4'82—dc22

                                                            2005012526

Published by Paulist Press
997 Macarthur Boulevard
Mahwah, New Jersey 07430

www.paulistpress.com

Printed and bound in the
United States of America

For my parents,
who helped me start the journey,

and for Matthew,
who has taught me so much about love

Contents

ACKNOWLEDGMENTS • ix

INTRODUCTION • 1

The First Dwelling Places • 19

The Second Dwelling Places • 29

The Third Dwelling Places • 37

The Fourth Dwelling Places • 47

The Fifth Dwelling Places • 61

The Sixth Dwelling Places • 77

The Seventh Dwelling Places • 111

WALKING WITH TERESA TODAY • 121

FOR FURTHER READING • 133

A TERESIAN CHRONOLOGY • 137

NOTES • 141

Acknowledgments

A BOOK LIKE THIS cannot be written without a great deal of prayerful accompaniment, and it is a true pleasure to be able to thank those whose conversations, prayers, and loving presence have guided me as I have conceptualized ideas and gradually found words to express them. First, of course, are the Xavier University students whose questions, perplexed frowns, insights, and energy have fueled my thoughts. I think, in particular, of my first undergraduate scholars seminar on Teresa in 1996 and of the powerful on-site study tour of Teresa in Spain during the summer of 2001 that brought so much of the text alive for us. I remember with gratitude and affection the wide circle of prayer that surrounded us on that trip, from Discalced Carmelites in Seville and Indiana to friends throughout the states; your support continues to provide food for the journey. The heart of this book was drafted shortly afterward, in the peaceful home of Paul and Mary Giles; their hospitality over the years has been a great blessing.

Collegial conversations have provided guidance and inspiration as well. In particular, I am grateful to William Madges, Rosie Miller, OFM, Paul Knitter, Elizabeth Groppe and Paul Lachance, OFM, for their insights and comments. Although time and space often keep us from the kinds of passionate exchanges that would have improved this work, I hope that this book responds worthily to the scholarship of Bernard McGinn, Alison Weber, and others whose thoughts have shaped my own, and I look forward to continuing such conversations in person. I would also like to thank the Jesuit community at Xavier

University for the research sabbatical that provided much-needed time for final revisions.

Graduate students in my class on Mysticism and Scripture in the summer of 2002 provided further motivation to move this work toward publication, and the beautiful red rocks of Sedona and moonlight walks on the floor of the Grand Canyon blessed me with their inspiring accompaniment as I prepared the final manuscript. I would like to express deep thanks to my undergraduate research assistant that summer, Lea Minniti, whose extraordinary range enabled her to collaborate in all the midwifery this manuscript required: from conversations, index searching, and proofreading to meditative walks, rock climbing, blister care, and even creativity with kale.

When I settled in to work on final revisions in January and February of 2003, gracefully bilocating from writing desk to meditations by the fireplace, a trapdoor fell open for me, unlocked by the guiding prayers of the most intimate companions of my soul. To you who have accompanied me on the internal journey that this book represents, I offer up both thanks beyond words for your loving companionship and my ongoing prayers that God will continue to guide us ever more deeply into the fiery mystery that burns so deeply in our hearts.

Introduction

*T*ERESA OF AVILA (1515–1582) is already known to many as one of the greatest Spanish mystics and a major figure in the Catholic Reformation of the sixteenth century, where she ranks in importance with Ignatius Loyola, the founder of the Jesuits, and the Jesuit missionary Francis Xavier, with whom she was canonized in 1622. Although historical circumstances denied her the more public reforming role that many of her male contemporaries enjoyed, Teresa nonetheless exerted a powerful influence from within the cloister, reforming the Carmelite order, founding convents throughout Spain, and moving medieval contemplative traditions into a new age through her mystical treatises. Clearly a gifted administrator, Teresa was able to manage the complex negotiations and social relations that establishing convents required, despite opposition from many fronts. But her truest vocation, as a writer, provided her with a powerful platform for the transformation of her world.

Declared a doctor of the Roman Catholic Church in 1970, Teresa has long been recognized as an astute spiritual director in her own right, and her books attest to her keen sensitivity to subjective states and the stages of spiritual growth. Her *Interior Castle*, in particular, could be understood as an attempt to capture the shifting landscapes of the psyche as it is touched by grace and commits itself to the transformative process that is the mystical journey. But, though Teresa accomplishes this impressive task, she achieves even more than that. As Bernard McGinn has cogently argued, using Teresa herself as a quintessential example, mystical experience ought not be separated from its theological meaning. As he warns: "Although it may be possi-

1

ble to make theoretical distinctions between mysticism and mystical theology, I believe it is dangerous to separate the two in the history of Christianity."[1] What appears to be, then, primarily Teresa's description of ever-deepening experiences of God is also and concurrently an evolving systematic theology, revealing insights into the nature of the human person, God, Christ, and the human–divine relationship.

To understand the *Interior Castle* properly, we must appreciate that it is both a spiritual classic and an important theological treatise, whose theological content has been, in some ways, "buried" both by rhetorical strategy and by Teresa's colloquial, personal tone. It is my hope that, in and through this "reader's guide," I can draw out the theological dimensions of this at times complex text and bridge what I see as an artificial gap between the pastoral and theological content of Teresa's *Interior Castle*. In this way I seek to facilitate both the comprehension and the application of Teresa's insights for modern readers.

The *Interior Castle* is a profound book, written by a passionate and insightful woman whose life continues to inspire those who have come to know her today, and it represents the culmination of an auspicious and prodigious writing career. Its very existence is rather remarkable, given the religious climate of sixteenth-century Spain. As many scholars have studied in detail, Teresa's status within church and society was at best precarious. She was a *conversa*, a woman, and a practitioner of mental prayer who defended the authenticity and authority of contemplation as a way to know God. These attributes left her vulnerable not only to social discrimination but, once she acquired a more public reputation for holiness, also to inquisitional investigation.

Scholars have been seeking to understand the full effects of Teresa's Jewish heritage ever since Alonso Cortes's publication, in 1946, of evidence demonstrating that her grandfather, Juan Sánchez de Cepeda, had been condemned as a practicing "judaizer" by the Inquisitional Tribunal of Toledo in 1485.[2] Teresa, quite naturally, makes no reference to this event, although she was certainly aware of it and lived, to some degree, under its shadow. She and her brothers adopted the surname Cepeda y Ahumada probably to avoid suspicion that the

Sánchez wing would generate; even still, they had to be creative to work around the strictures of *limpieza de sangre* ("purity of blood") that denied descendents of Jewish ancestors social rights and benefits, including access to public office and certain religious orders.[3] Many *conversos* maintained significant economic influence, and Christian institutions, including Teresa's own discalced reform, often relied on financial support from wealthy *converso* merchants.[4] Teresa's own experiences of the hypocritical ecclesiastical and social treatment of *conversos* in sixteenth-century Spain probably adds an extra edge to her many criticisms of worldly honor and esteem (see, e.g., *Life* 2:3–6; 11:2; 13:4; 20:26; 27:17).

Juan Sánchez reestablished himself in Avila by 1493, where he achieved commercial success in the cloth trade, and by 1500 he had acquired a *pleito de hidalguía*, entitling him to the status of gentleman and exemption from taxes. When Teresa was born, on March 28, 1515, she entered a family whose wealth and business connections afforded her and her siblings a certain protection from overt discrimination; Teresa's portrayal of her early years—tailored, perhaps, to hide her *converso* origins—indicates that she was raised within a devout Catholic environment. When her mother died in 1528, Teresa was thirteen years old. Her older sister married soon afterward, and Teresa was surrounded by brothers and cousins who may not have been the best influence on her. Her father sent her to the Augustinian convent of Nuestra Señora de la Gracia as a boarding student. This was a small, austere convent, and, while Teresa was impressed with the virtue of the nun in charge of novices and boarders, María de Briceño, she felt no great religious vocation, even as she began to pray to God for guidance as to her future (*Life* 3:20). It took several years and recovery from serious illness for Teresa to determine that she would enter a convent, encouraged, as she describes, by the *Letters of St. Jerome*. She entered the Carmelite convent of the Encarnación on November 2, 1535, and made her profession there a year later.

The Encarnación was a large convent, housing over one hundred nuns, and the kinds of class distinctions that pervaded society also characterized the women there. At the Encarnación, Teresa had a private apartment with facilities for cooking and eating, large enough to house her and, at times, a female relative. While Teresa was probably comfortable in her new residence, the convent itself could not provide adequately for all the nuns, many of whom were encouraged to return to their families for meals during the day. Indeed, the convent seemed to be the hub of many social activities, and Teresa describes lively conversations in the convent parlor that she later regretted as frivolous (*Life* 7:1–5). Subsequent reflection on her early convent years led Teresa to conclude that enclosure and more intimate religious communities were necessary for successful immersion into the contemplative vocation (*Life* 7:3).

Despite her relatively comfortable circumstances, Teresa reports that adapting to convent life took a physical toll on her (*Life* 4:5). After her first year in the convent, her father arranged for her to be taken to a doctor in Becedas for special attention. These cures helped little, and she returned to the convent, continuing to suffer infirmities including nausea, heart pains, fainting spells and nerve pains (*Life* 5:7-9). In August 1539, she was unconscious for four days and nearly given up for dead (*Life* 5:9). It took her three years to regain her strength and to learn to walk again. In retrospect, she relates that these experiences taught her a great deal about prayer and virtue, and some of the witnesses for her canonization say that her desire to reform the Carmelite order was born in these years.

During Lent of 1554 an experience of contrition, facilitated by a statue of the wounded Christ, caused her to dedicate herself more deeply to the path of mental prayer. As her experiences of prayer intensified, she became even more determined to establish a proper context for contemplative devotion, and she began to consult with new spiritual directors, including several Jesuits who had recently settled into a new foundation in Avila.[5] The more she dedicated herself to this prayerful life, the more she learned about God and the more she felt the need for religious reform. Teresa's experiences of mental prayer included several supernatural experiences that she found difficult to put into words, causing her to consult with spiritual experts and to read literature on prayer. A passionate and committed student,

Teresa became as theologically literate as most of her university educated male peers.

With respect to her spiritual and theological formation, Teresa took inspiration from the extensive tradition of Christian hagiography, available in collections of saints' lives. She also knew and appreciated earlier authors within the Christian theological tradition, including Augustine, Jerome, Gregory the Great, and Catherine of Siena. Further, she consulted extensively with theologians throughout Spain, including some she knew would not be sympathetic to the range of her spiritual experiences.[6] She learned from the prayer techniques and incarnational theology of the Franciscan school, represented in Spain by such authors as Francisco de Osuna and Bernardino de Laredo, and she was highly influenced by other writers of the *spirituales* school, which strove to make the mystical tradition of contemplative prayer more accessible to readers of the vernacular. Thus, scholars have noted similarities between her works and Juan de Avila's *Audi filia,* Luis de Granada's *Libro de la oración,* and Pedro de Alcántara's *Avisos y reglas.* These authors taught techniques of recollection in which individuals turned away from external distractions to seek God within the heart. Their teaching involved internal quieting and focused meditation on the passion of Christ.

But Teresa's search to learn techniques of mental prayer was in some ways limited by the appearance of the Valdés Index of Prohibited Books in 1559.[7] The Index contained books written by some of the more important spiritual authors of Teresa's day, including Juan de Avila and Luis de Granada. At the heart of the controversy was the extent to which mental prayer, with its focus on the internal life of the Spirit and the individual's partnership with God, was compatible with the sacramental and institutional life of the church. After the Council of Trent (1545–1562), the Roman Catholic Church adopted a more catechetical approach to Christianity, focusing its efforts on teaching basic doctrine and encouraging the laity in the rosary and other forms of vocal prayer. Within Spain, often heralded as one of the "most Catholic" countries, this orientation to basic forms of piety was perhaps more pronounced than in some other countries.[8] Nevertheless, the late sixteenth century saw a veritable flowering of mystics such as Teresa, John of the Cross, Luis de León, and others, all of whom attempted, around the strictures of institutional scrutiny, to express the reality of the God they experienced to their contemporaries.

Institutional suspicion of mental prayer had two very real implications for Teresa. First, she would have to defend herself when challenged by some of her contemporaries who were concerned that her experiences were not authentic (*Life* chaps. 28–30). Second, her evolving vision of reform within the Carmelite order was predicated on a corps of informed, prayerful women. Yet the Index now banned some of the books Teresa and her nuns needed to sustain their spiritual growth. Deprived of them, how would women entering the contemplative life be able to learn mental prayer and live out their religious vocation? As she relates in her *Life,* Teresa offered the dilemma to God in prayer and was answered: "Do not be troubled. I will give you a living book" (26:5). The double implication of this exchange was that Teresa herself would begin to embody mental prayer in her person and that she could, through the book of her *Life,* fill the void in formative spiritual literature caused by the Index. At about this same time, after Teresa had consulted with many spiritual experts, she began to compose an account of her spiritual experiences in order that these experts could ascertain their authenticity. In this account she described repeated reassurances she received directly from God about the authenticity of her prayer experiences as well as experiences that made scripture literally come alive for her; she began to understand that she was receiving theological insights directly from God. All of these experiences compelled her to write her *Life,* first composed in 1562 and then revised in 1565. Teresa's deepest vocation, as a mystical theologian, had finally crystallized.

Over the course of her life Teresa would write four major books—the *Life; The Way of Perfection,* a manual of prayer for the Discalced Carmelites under her care; *The Book of Foundations,* an account of her activities as the reformer of the Carmelite order; and *The Interior Castle*—and many other works, including monastic documents, brief accounts of her individual spiritual experiences, poetry, and letters (some 450 of them extant). However, the circulation of Teresa's works was greatly limited, given the climate of inquisitional review.[9] Teresa's works were not published until 1588, six years after her death, and their public appearance set in motion theological debate that took over a decade to resolve.[10] By that time, however, Teresa's gifts as a writer had already been much appreciated by contemporaries who testified to the capacity of her works to inspire moral and spiritual conversion in their readers. Indeed, many, like Luis de León, editor of her *Complete Works*, were convinced that Teresa's writings were miraculous productions, capable themselves of communicating the divine to their readers.[11] A prime example of general conviction about the miraculous nature of Teresa's writing is the image of Teresa writing in ecstasy, face illuminated, first perpetuated by members of her religious communities[12] and later by artists who incorporated rays of light and/or a dove over Teresa's head into the standard seventeenth-century iconography of the saint. Such imagery was intended to reinforce the belief that the Holy Spirit had inspired, perhaps even dictated, the books.[13] For centuries this instrumental view of Teresa prevailed, as commentators on Teresa's works maintained that Teresa lacked originality, added few theological insights to the Christian tradition, and wrote primarily, even exclusively, out of obedience.

However, as Alison Weber notes in her *Teresa of Avila and the Rhetoric of Femininity,* our understanding of Teresa as a writer took important turns with the publication of Victor García de la Concha's *El arte literario de Santa Teresa* in 1978. Building on the historical research of the previous several decades, which showed that Teresa made conscious and careful choices as an author, García de la Concha reviewed Teresa's literary formation and argued that she was able to express herself through a mystical language for women that was appropriate, accessible, and informative because of her rhetorical skill. But it was Weber herself who explored with careful detail how Teresa's colloquial style was related to "the pragmatics of writing as a woman in Counter-Reformation Spain," concluding that Teresa "created a discourse that was at once public and private, didactic and affiliative, authoritative and familiar."[14] Indeed, as I have argued elsewhere, the complexity of self-representation in Teresa's prose allowed her to develop and sustain a theological voice despite her limitations as an "unlettered woman" without ecclesiastical authority.[15]

The very strength of Teresa's rhetoric, which won her acceptance and endorsement as a canonized saint and, eventually, as a doctor of the Roman Catholic Church, has continued to disguise her work as a theologian. For we have still underestimated Teresa's theological creativity, as Rowan Williams notes:

> Teresa of Avila is one of the most accessible and attractive of all the great writers in the Christian mystical tradition; but her very human attractiveness and the fascination of her unusual experiences of vision and rapture tend to obscure two salient facts about her. First, she was a woman reacting to a particularly difficult epoch in the history of the Spanish state and Church; and second, she was an independent theological thinker.[16]

Yet such independence was frowned upon even in Teresa's male contemporaries; thus Teresa disguised carefully her entrance into the domain of theological discourse, as it raised many issues of theological and ecclesiastical authority.[17]

The appearance of a recent comparative study, *John of the Cross and Teresa of Avila: Mystical Knowing and Selfhood* by Edward Howells, changes much of this picture.[18] This study gives Teresa the theological attention she deserves and, by exploring the connections among Teresa's understanding of the self, her changing epistemology, her Christology and her reflection on the nature of God, provides important insights in furthering our understanding of Teresa's theological contributions to the Christian mystical tradition. Howells's examination of the ways in which Teresa's theology evolved over the course of her mystical life leads him to conclude that her understanding of the transformation of the self through the mystical life entailed a growing apprehension of the dynamic nature of God expressed in the Trinity. My work on the stages of growth in the soul's self-knowledge, the soul's changing epistemology and the growing depth of the soul's relationship with God described in Teresa's *Interior Castle* has led me to the same conclusion. Although Howells and I differ slightly in our understanding of Teresa's ultimate conclusions on the nature of the soul—particularly, whether the soul is characterized more primarily by an inherent division or an inherent unity—naivete about Teresa's theological prowess is no longer possible. As we sharpen our analysis of Teresa's responses to the historical realities of her day and seek to understand more carefully the choices she made as woman of outstanding intelligence, common sense, determination, and integrity, perhaps we can now recognize, particularly through the *Interior Castle*, her great talent not just as a rhetorician but as a *theological doctor*. Further, we can affirm that one of her unique gifts as a theologian rests in her ability to create and shape a narrative interpretation of personal experience that reveals to readers the reality of a God who is active in human life and engages us to see the presence of God in our own life journeys.

As we saw before, Teresa began to understand her vocation as a theologian as a direct result of the appearance of the Valdés Index of Prohibited Books, and thus, as Antonio Márquez declares: "The works of St. Teresa cannot be explained genetically without the action of the Inquisition."[19] Ironically, the operation of the Inquisition was at once, for Teresa, both a stimulus to write and an obstacle to write around. The potential charge of heresy affected the many choices Teresa made as an author.[20]

It is difficult to assess accurately the effects of the Spanish Inquisition on the theological climate of sixteenth-century Spain. Although the Inquisition as an institution sought to promote social, political, and religious unity by imposing and enforcing doctrinal uniformity, its activity actually served, at times, as an impetus for change and resistance; therefore, it is not completely correct to think of the climate in sixteenth-century Spain as intrinsically repressive. The Inquisition, originally established in 1478 in an attempt to monitor the orthodoxy of Jewish people who had converted to Christianity, had, by the mid-sixteenth century, expanded its jurisdiction considerably.[21] After the expulsion of Jews from Spain in 1492, the Inquisition became a means to control religious culture, particularly the discussion and circulation of religious ideas, and to enforce certain doctrines and codes of ritual and ethical conduct. Thus, most Catholics who acquired some kind of public religious role, particularly if they taught about prayer and the mystical life, underwent inquisitional scrutiny during their lifetime. Ignatius of Loyola, for example, was investigated by the Inquisition three times early in his religious career, and Teresa herself faced inquisitional review in Seville in 1576 after suspicions were raised about her *Life* before several inquisitional tribunals.

One of the greatest challenges spiritual teachers faced during this time was inquisitional suspicion of mental prayer, which seemed to threaten the sacramental life of the church and the authority of ecclesiastical officials. Accusations against *alumbradismo,* or false mysticism, while not as numerous or as common as accusations made against Lutherans, judaizers, or *moriscos* (practicing Muslims), provide important insight into the history of religiosity and theology in sixteenth-century Spain. We can observe several waves of prosecution of *alumbrados* (false mystics), first in the 1520s and 1530s, then again in the 1570s, and finally in the 1610s and 1620s.[22] The first wave corresponds to concerns over the infiltration of Lutheran ideas into the Iberian Peninsula, for the Protestant Reformation fueled fears that those who made claims to religious experiences might use their charismatic authority in ways that would undermine church doctrines or institutional structures. By 1525 inquisitors had begun to define *alumbradismo* but viewed it primarily as a lack of respect for the sacraments, veneration of the saints, rituals, and institutional structures of the church. Many of the *alumbrados* prosecuted during the 1520s were concurrently accused of Lutheran beliefs. However, their dedication to inner forms of religiosity, including mental prayer and, particularly, a form of contemplation called *dexamiento,* was noted with concern.

By the 1550s, a more concerted effort to regulate and impose limits on individual speculation and prayer practices had emerged, resulting most powerfully in the Valdés Index of Prohibited Books, but also exemplified in the appearance of treatises actively discouraging mental prayer or teaching the discernment of spirits. It is here that we must return to our examination of Teresa's life as a female theologian operating under the shadow of the Index, whose *Life* testified to a number of embodied supernatural experiences that raised questions about their nature.[23] The fact that throughout the 1560s Teresa also founded several convents that relied on public support placed her in an even more precarious position. Indeed, her first foundation, the convent of San José, established in Avila in August of 1562, triggered threats of inquisitorial investigation from townspeople angered that the discalced (i.e., "shoeless" or reformed) nuns would live in poverty and require the support of the faithful.[24]

In the 1570s, having now achieved a public presence, both through her reform efforts and the popularity of her writing, Teresa encountered more challenges to her expressions of religiosity.[25] In 1575 the Valladolid tribunal of the Inquisition ordered a theological review of the *Life* for orthodoxy. Although the censor, the Dominican Domingo Bañez, knew Teresa personally, had given her spiritual direction, and could vouch for her sincerity, his recommendation to the inquisitional tribunal indicated his discomfort with the public circulation of the *Life*, because it contained "many revelations and visions, which should always be feared, especially in women, who are more likely to believe they come from God and to see holiness in them." Bañez suggested that the book was "not suitable for just anyone to read, but for learned men, experienced and of Christian discretion."[26] As a result of Bañez's recommendations, the original manuscript of the *Life* was held by the inquisitional tribunal, and Teresa was never able to secure its return to her.

At the same time that her *Life* was under review in Valladolid, Teresa was engaged in the foundation of a new discalced convent in Seville, where she and her nuns encountered opposition both from the non-reformed (Calced) Carmelites and from the inquisitional tribunal there. The nuns were accused of moral misconduct, including sexual immorality and suspicious devotional practices. In February and March 1576 Teresa wrote formal statements about her practice of mental prayer which the tribunal reviewed.[27] Although the tribunal in Seville did not pursue charges against Teresa, she was ordered by her Carmelite superiors to choose a convent and stay there in reclusion. As usual, Teresa found obedience a very flexible virtue; after settling into Toledo, she had conversations with her confessor, Jerónimo Gracián, and expressed concerns about the fate of her *Life*. Gracián then "ordered" her in early 1577 to rewrite the *Life* in the third person. Recalling this exchange later, Gracián wrote:

> Being her confessor and speaking with her once in Toledo about many things concerning her spirit, she said to me: "Oh, how well that point is written in the book of my life, which the Inquisition has!" And I said to her: "Well, since we can't recover it, write down what you remember, and other things, and write another book, and explain the basic doctrine without identifying the person who has experienced what you say there.…[28]

Teresa went far beyond Gracián's command, as the resulting treatise, her *Interior Castle,* is no mere recasting of the *Life* but rather a dense and mature theological piece. Its careful defense of mystical prayer, visions, rapture, and the doctrine of union with God can be viewed only as a bold counter-response to inquisitional scrutiny of "false mystics."[29] All too keenly aware of both the internal and external obstacles faced by those dedicated to contemplation and the search for God, Teresa wrote the *Interior Castle* to offer her companions in prayer a compass for their theological and spiritual journey.

Teresa was clearly a consummate spiritual director, a role she had, at times, to assume for herself and which she also exercised as abbess in many of her foundations. In the *Interior Castle* she describes the mystical journey as an internal progression of seven stages leading to union with God. Each stage entails growth in self-knowledge and a maturing vision of the self and God. Spiritual insights and sensitive exploration of the subjective realm abound throughout the *Interior Castle,* and perhaps Teresa's descriptive gifts in this arena have kept us from fully appreciating her contributions as a theologian, for we tend to see experiential narratives as being "spiritual," not "theological." This is an artificial distinction, as many scholars have noted, and Edward Howells's recent study goes a great distance toward bridging it. As Howells argues, Teresa uses the word *experience* to mean "apprehended knowledge";[30] thus we should consider her narration of experiences of God as a form of constructive theology, in which she gradually finds words to express the reality of God revealed through her increasing consciousness of God's presence.[31] This makes her work an important corrective to the "divorce" of spirituality and theology that began shortly after her death.[32] For as we shall see, the *Interior Castle*'s insights on human nature and the nature of God, mediated through the evolving self, are of the same quality and depth of those of Christian thinkers like Origen, Augustine, Bernard of Clairvaux, Bonaventure, Meister Eckhart, and Julian of Norwich—whose perspectives on God and human nature continue to guide and shape theology today. Indeed, the *Interior Castle* should be appreciated as one of the best examples of a text that functions at autobiographical, didactic, reflective, metaphorical, speculative and anagogical levels, demonstrating the inherent connections among them.

The fifteen years that separate Teresa's *Interior Castle* from her *Life* involved considerable spiritual and theological maturation. Teresa's continually deepening experience of mystical union and the concurrent forms of knowing it opened up for her led her to a theological synthesis she could not have reached in the 1560s. Theological evolution is evident in her understandings of mystical union, of God, of Christ, and of the human person. Edward Howells has begun the process of describing some of the developments in Teresa's thought,[33] and, although we still await a definitive presentation of Teresa's systematic theology, the significantly more complex ideas, language, and theological method of her *Interior Castle* lead me to conclude that its theological views supersede her earlier views, without invalidating them. Indeed, they show the same kind of theological deepening and ripening as do the two versions of *Showings* written by the English mystic Julian of Norwich (d. c. 1423), first in about 1373 and then in about 1393.[34] On a theological level, then, what Teresa writes in the *Life,* the *Way of Perfection,* and other works should be checked against comparable passages in the *Interior Castle* before assuming that it represents her final word as a theologian. This is not to suggest that her other works make lesser intellectual and literary contributions; indeed, even at the level of narrative theology Teresa accomplishes some things in her earlier works that are lost in the synthesis of the *Interior Castle.*

Ideally, to understand Teresa well, and certainly to observe the profound transformation she experienced through mystical union, one should at least read both her *Life* and her *Interior Castle.* The theological development that the two works reflect is expressed most directly in the changed perspective on humanity and human life that the books represent. When Teresa went back to "rewrite" the lost *Life,* as Gracián claims he suggested, she did not simply reject the first-person narrative style of the *Life,* changing its voice to a third-person analytical style, although, given the circumstances of her inquisitional investigation, it is easy to see why she did. More importantly, the generic difference of the two texts represents the divinely informed perspectival differences gained through her years in prayer. The *Life* is a narrative account of a soul's journey recounted through individual experiences; in it, Teresa uses the chronology of events to describe her growing awareness of God's presence and activity in her life. Rooted in the flow of human events and human interactions is a section on prayer in which Teresa reflects on the soul as a garden in which the connection between God and the human person is forged and God's grace allows for greater human flourishing and moments of union with God. The *Interior Castle,* on the other hand, is Teresa's relation of her interior life ordered not by quantitative experiences of God but by her soul's qualitative progression toward union with God. The structure of this journey, its own organic life separable from the human events that had led Teresa to see divine activity in her life, and the fitting together of experiences with their ontological meanings, were impossible for her to see and express while she was in the very midst of the transformations they were accomplishing. The patterns of her experiences and the theological lessons learned had to be woven together over time through the habit of contemplation and from the perspective gained through union with God.

The *Interior Castle* is a richly evocative tapestry of metaphors, integrated scriptural references, and Teresa's own spiritual experiences, a work that both incarnates a profound theological worldview and invites its readers to live more deeply in that reality. Conceptualizing the soul as an intricate castle made of diamond or crystal within which God dwells, Teresa encourages us to explore the richness of our interior depths, and reinforces the essential goodness of the soul created in the image of God. This image provides an important contrast to the image of the garden, which had served as the primary metaphor for the soul in her *Life*, one that highlighted the dynamic nature of the self but did not highlight so strongly the depths of union the soul experiences in and with God because of inherent similarity to God. These images do not contradict each other, but have different points of departure and should be read together so that their perspectives can inform each other.

Indeed, the perspectival difference of these two metaphors of the soul, when placed together in this way, appears to replicate the perspectival difference of the two creation accounts in Genesis. The first account depicts the orderly creation of the cosmos, culminating in the origin of humanity, created in the image of God. The formlessness of the creating God reinforces the transcendence of the divine; the only hint that humanity has of God's identity is through the divine image replicated in humanity. The second creation account, portrays a much more immanent God, who reaches into the soil to form and shape Adam out of material that is wholly other than God, animating it with God's own breath. Through the metaphor of the soul as garden in the *Life*, Teresa suggests that the flourishing of the human person depends on the water of God's grace, which nurtures and sustains all life. Humanity inherits the task of gardening, sharing with Christ, the prototypical gardener, in the tasks of weeding and watering. Progressively over the course of a lifetime, the soul eliminates what is potentially destructive to its well-being, cultivating a deeper relationship with

God and receiving more direct communications of God's love. Visions and brief forms of ecstatic union with God characterize the end of the *Life;* they are of the kind that, in the *Interior Castle,* are characteristic of the soul's preparations for union with God in its deepest center.

Toward the end of the *Life,* in her first attempt to articulate the relationship between God and the soul, Teresa approaches the diamond and crystal analogy, an image she suggests is revealed to her over the course of several visionary experiences, but at this time she is not able to say more than that it appears that Christ and the soul somehow mirror each other.[35] However, Teresa is so stunned by the brilliance of Christ, whom she sees in the center of the soul, that she cannot imagine any reconciliation between the splendor of the divine in the soul and the "ugly" state of humanity soiled and stained by sin. She expresses the dichotomy in strongly self-condemnatory language:

> It is most saddening, each time I recall, to see appearing in that pure brilliance things as ugly as were my sins. It happens that whenever I recall this, I fail to know how I can bear it; as a result I am then left with such shame that I don't think I know where to hide. (*Life* 40:10)

But a more reconciled understanding of the divine–human relationship, facilitated by the fifteen years of mystical experience that separates the two books, is apparent in the *Interior Castle,* which opens with a much more sophisticated presentation of the crystal metaphor as its point of departure.

Structuring the story of her soul around significant metaphors, as she does throughout the *Interior Castle,* illustrates the kind of metaphorical thinking that had led Teresa to deeper insights into the nature of God and a divinely informed worldview. As the text demonstrates, revelatory or mystical "sight" is an integrative way of thinking, where perception through metaphor, scripture, and analogy allow the human person to think beyond the empirical and to expand his or her understanding of reality. We have not yet developed a real definition of "mystical knowing" that allows us to "see" from the perspective of our growing consciousness of the presence of God. But Teresa's careful documentation of the kinds of subjective transformation she herself experienced gives us clues to what happens as we learn to live consciously within the presence of God. Certainly, one of her greatest gifts as a writer is her ability to express the depths of her subjective experiences of self and God, seeking, through words, both to express the reality of the immensely tender and awe-inspiring God she knew and to draw her readers into that reality. Recognizing a certain experiential wisdom and authenticity in her prose, we can explore the theological insights offered as she reveals, in her own naked soul-searching, her concurrent growing consciousness of the presence of God within and all around her.

Teresa's ability to speak through the centuries and present us, even today, with a brilliant sketch of the inner landscape of the human psyche, is perhaps the clearest indication of her theological talent. While the *Interior Castle* has been much studied by those seeking to understand human spiritual development, readers have failed to appreciate fully the power and profundity of the theological insights—insights into the very nature of God and humanity—she offers, precisely because she has plumbed her own depths with such thoroughness, integrity, and emotional authenticity.[36]

If we have failed to fathom and integrate fully Teresa's theological contributions, this may be because her knowledge of God in self, other, and world becomes approachable only with a holistic way of knowing—through the senses, through the imagination, through the intellect, and through the awakened soul. Exploring the theological dimensions of the text, then, will require more effort of us as readers than what we typically give a book. Rather than moving rapidly from concept to concept, engaging in abstract examination, we will have to move slowly and meditatively through the *Interior Castle*, in order to engage more fully with the realities made possible in words that are felt and experienced as deeply true. We will have to apply her ideas to our own life experiences in order to probe their truth with patience, and, out of such reflection, we can then also explore both the more universal and the more practical applications of her theological insights. For thinking *with*, not merely thinking *through*, the *Interior Castle* has, potentially, a cumulative and even transformative effect on the reader. Thus, it is a book that bears many readings and that encourages us to read our own souls along with it. Other reflective techniques, such as journaling, reading aloud, or reading in community, may also help us to slow down and move more readily into the flow of insights contained in the book. Enabling that kind of reading, one of full engagement, is the purpose of this work, which is meant to be read alongside the *Interior Castle*, both to interpret the text and to help it come alive for us in the twenty-first century.

The
First
Dwelling
Places

*T*HE *INTERIOR CASTLE* is first and foremost a descriptive and prescriptive itinerary toward union with God, a God encountered, discovered, and revealed gradually in the innermost recesses of the soul.[1] This simple declaration already contains a number of powerful theological assertions, including perhaps the most provocative invitation for reflection: that to be fully human, a true self, is to grow into a way of living out the reality of God-with-us. Such an exalted vision of human life may seem preposterous from the particularity of our numerous human perspectives; it is a worldview that must, perhaps, be taken "on faith" at the outset, but it is certainly a compelling worldview, with the power to transform not only our ways of thinking and knowing but our ways of being. Its very truth begins to demonstrate itself in and through introspection, meditation, and contemplation.[2]

Such is Teresa of Avila's proposition to her readers at the outset of the *Interior Castle,* a treatise divided into seven sections, or "dwelling places,"[3] each one representing a further stage of development in the realization and integration of the fullness of the human being. The idea that the soul consists of mansions or "dwelling places" comes from the Gospel of John, in which Christ says, "In my Father's house are many mansions; if it were not so, would I have told you that I go to prepare a place for you? And when I go and prepare a place for you, I will come again and will take you to myself, that where I am you may be also" (John 14:2–3). For Teresa, Christ's allusion was not only to an "external" world that we might imagine as heaven but also to the rich "internal" world of the soul. Thus she offers us a clear vision of the human person, a theological anthropology that allows us to explore what it might mean when scripture asserts that the human person was created in the image and likeness of God (Gen. 1:26). For Teresa, exploration of the self will reveal that likeness within the soul's own depths, enticing it into deeper relationship with the divine potential embedded within it.

A wisened traveler herself,[4] Teresa knew that she could not provide a roadmap for such a journey without first describing the destination, in order to motivate readers to undertake the arduous trip. In the first dwelling places of the *Interior Castle*, then, Teresa presents her readers with an overview of the soul's journey toward union with God by way of metaphors that express her understanding of human nature and the God–human relationship. At the same time, she invites readers to begin this journey into the depths or "center" of their own interiors through the gateway of prayer. The framework for the soul's journey inward is introduced at the outset of the work, a blending of John's mansions and the metaphor of a crystal or diamond. Teresa begins her work by writing:

> Today while I was beseeching our Lord to speak for me because I wasn't able to think of anything to say nor did I know how to begin to carry out this obedience, there came to my mind what I shall now speak about, that which will provide us with a basis to begin with. It is that we consider our soul to be like a castle made entirely out of a diamond or of very clear crystal, in which there are many rooms, just as in heaven there are many dwelling places. (I:1:1)[5]

As she describes individual rooms in this castle, Teresa seems to suggest that they are like concentric spheres, gradually leading into a single chamber, the depths of the soul where God dwells.

> Let us consider that this castle has, as I said, many dwelling places: some up above, others down below, others to the sides; and in the center and middle is the main dwelling place where the very secret exchanges between God and the soul take place. (I:1:3)

Exploring this interior castle of the soul, then, involves moving through the spaces of the psyche, gradually arriving at a more authentic knowledge of self and, concurrently, coming to know the God who resides in that center. In order to reinforce that process, Teresa layers another metaphor over those of the crystal and the castle, explaining that the castle's dwelling places are arranged concentrically in layers, like a palmetto plant or an artichoke.

> You mustn't think of these dwelling places in such a way that each one would follow in file after the other; but turn your eyes toward the center, which is the room or royal chamber where the King stays, and think of how a palmetto has many leaves surrounding and covering the tasty part that can be eaten. (I:1:8)

Embedded in her structural metaphors is Teresa's argument that our personhood is sacred, a treasure of inestimable worth, partly because it was created by God and partly because, as God's creation, it contains God in its deepest center. Unfortunately, however, as she continues to observe, "we seldom consider the precious things that can be found in this soul, or who dwells within it, or its high value. Consequently, little effort is made to preserve its beauty" (I:1:2). What Teresa appears to lament here is the lack of consideration we pay to life and to ourselves. It is as if, she suggests, we do not know how to dwell deeply within ourselves; instead, we spend ourselves in movement from activity to activity. Absorbed in superficial movement in the world around us, we lack genuine engagement with ourselves, our internal senses and our intuitions, and therefore do not know how to "activate" the divine life within us.

To come to know and appreciate the treasures of our inner recesses entails, then, a process of exploration and peeling, a stripping away of the protective layers of selfhood that enable us to survive in the world around us but at the same time keep us from the depths of our soft, vulnerable heart, where, Teresa promises, God resides eternally. In this conflation of metaphors of castle, crystal, and palmetto plant, Teresa has integrated the need to defend the "treasure" of the soul against adversarial forces with the suggestion that vulnerability, tenderness, and blissful union are qualities essential to fullness of life.

Coming to know and appreciate ourselves as soulful people is critical to understanding any truth about God or the human person and to finding or creating a meaningful life. If our external circumstances do not remind us of that reality and reinforce it for us, we run the risk of internalizing a distorted sense of self. As Teresa suggests, perhaps more implicitly here, and certainly explicitly by the second and third dwelling places where she discusses the need for spiritual companionship, the context for authentic self-discovery and identity-building is critical, for others play a large role in helping us define who we are.

In the first dwelling places, Teresa is calling us toward a temporary stillness to consider the purpose of our lives and to move us into deeper purposefulness. If we begin to understand ourselves as dwelling places of God, we can then take more seriously the possibility that our life, our selfhood, and our relationships with others are all sacred spaces to be cultivated.[6] Interestingly, however, this stillness with respect to the external world is combined with a kind of purposeful, prayerful movement through the expanses of the inner world; this kind of movement both replicates and enables God's active, not merely static, presence within ourselves.[7] In and through this exploratory process we catch the first glimpses of our deepest nature as children of God, and this new vision of our created potential— knowledge of our own souls—is intended to raise for us the question: What informs our primary consciousness of who we are? Living out of that deeper nature is perhaps more difficult than we realize. Often our understanding of our personhood has been derived primarily from what others have taught us about ourselves, from our social norms and values, or from the *personas* we develop in any number of interpersonal and professional spheres. In other words, we typically live disconnected from the deeper sense of personhood that can transcend our existential circumstances. This lack of recognition of our own soulfulness reinforces and is reinforced by our tendency not to engage in proper care of the soul, our own or others'. Further, our sense of worth as persons is equally bound up in such superficial self-knowledge, so that our orientation to appearances—physical appearance, social status, professional standing, or any of the other spheres that define our selfhood—can keep us from the experiential knowledge of our own depths and capacities or distort our perception of the deeper and more critical reality of God's ongoing and even immediate presence in our lives.

Lack of accomplishment in any of these major spheres of our lives—professional, familial, interpersonal, physical—can have profound effects on how we understand ourselves, even of who we understand ourselves to be. At times, even the pursuit of goals that are themselves noble and good can drive us to adopt behavioral patterns that threaten our essential well-being, as so often happens with stress-induced types of illnesses. We can also become overly absorbed in the emotional drama of our lives, getting caught up in anger, jealousy, anxiety, or other feelings that keep us from the process of stripping away what is unnecessary or ineffective. In this way emotions become distractions in and of themselves, yet another way to avoid monotony, pain, or the incompletion we may feel before we begin to deepen our own personal integrity and authenticity.

For many of us, our lives are entangled in relationships, responsibilities, and desires that pull us into complex logistical situations. "Managing" the many spheres of work, home, relational and familial development makes it difficult to attend to the growth of our internal spirit. But disconnection from the primary responsibility of care of the soul, as the ground out of which all other cares proceed smoothly and effectively, can lead to personal disintegration and even a confused, disoriented relationship to one's self, another reflection of our lack of recognition of our own value. For Teresa, this faulty prioritizing is akin to confusing the diamond with its setting.[8] Further, it reflects a lack of vision of our own grandeur. Teresa encourages us to know ourselves in our fullness. She writes:

> The things of the soul must always be considered as plentiful, spacious, and large; to do so is not an exaggeration. The soul is capable of much more than we can imagine, and the sun that is in this royal chamber shines in all parts. (I:2:8)

Indeed, lack of recognition of the soul's grandeur is a symptom, for Teresa, of original sin, and our actions in this state of unawareness contribute to the further "blackening" of the crystal that is our soul, as if it were thrown into a puddle of muddy water, obscuring its true identity. Although the shining sun that represents God "is always present in the soul, and nothing can take away its loveliness…if a black cloth is placed over a crystal that is in the sun, obviously the sun's brilliance will have no effect on the crystal even though the sun is shining on it" (I:2:2). Our lack of soulful self-knowledge, then, causes the diamond that is the soul to plant itself "in a place where the water is black and foul smelling, [so that] everything that flows from it is equally wretched and filthy" (I:2:2). To see the ultimate misfortune of such a soul is to see concurrently the need for an orientation to ultimate reality, or God.

In the second chapter of the first dwelling places, Teresa refers to a vision of a soul in mortal sin, using the third person to disguise herself: "I know a person to whom our Lord wanted to show what a soul in mortal sin was like" (I:2:2).[9] This experience had lasting effects, causing Teresa both to fear offending God and to see that whatever good she accomplished was not completely of her own doing. In other words, understanding of the human capacity to err and sin leads the soul to cultivate a deeper relationship with God through the virtue of humility. For Teresa, humility does not mean self-abasement so much as an appreciation of our constant fallibility and our need for support in our desire for goodness. Humility, or proper self-knowledge with respect to God, frees us to move into our created potential by reaching out for divine assistance whenever we fall short on our own. In other words, humility enables a deeper extension of the self, empowered by God, as Teresa writes: "Believe me, we shall practice much better virtue through God's help than by being tied down to our own misery." And she asserts, "While we are on this earth nothing is more important to us than humility" (I:2:8–9). The liberating power of humility is personified in Christ, who is our model, both in learning humility and in understanding self-transcendence. Teresa writes:

> We should set our eyes on Christ, our Good, and on His saints. There we shall learn true humility, the intellect will be

enhanced, as I have said, and self-knowledge will not make one base and cowardly. (I:2:11)

Despite the confusion and obscurity that humans experience through sin, Teresa wants, ultimately, to convey that sin and its darkness are contrary to the soul's created capacity. She affirms: "[A]lthough the very sun that gave the soul so much brilliance and beauty is still in the center, the soul is as though it were not there to share in these things. Yet, it is as capable of enjoying His Majesty as is crystal capable of reflecting the sun's brilliance" (I:2:1). Thus, recognition of its fallen nature serves as the impetus for the soul to open itself to the possibility of a deeper, created potentiality, knowable through its own journey toward self-discovery.

For Teresa, true self-knowledge is rooted in the concurrent knowledge of God-in-self, as she observes, "We shall never completely know ourselves if we don't strive to know God" (I:2:9). And this kind of dedicated self-knowledge involves a gradual letting go of "unnecessary things and business affairs...in conformity with one's state in life" (I:2:14). For these extraneous cares can ensnare us and make it impossible for us even to enjoy ourselves, our lives, and our relationships with others as children of God. Their toxic effect on our self-knowledge is powerful; they provide us with occasions to sin, and Teresa characterizes them as "snakes and vipers and poisonous creatures that enter [into the castle] with the soul and don't allow it to be aware of the light" (I:2:14).

Even though Teresa's readers were not likely to be mired in the grasp of "mortal sin," Teresa suggests that all of us reach points at which we can be overcome by the confusing tangle of lives constructed around our reactions to external events. In that state it is common to respond to others in ways that belie our capacity to be peacefully and compassionately present to them. But there is a straightforward way out of such a tangle: to recall who we truly are by beginning to spend time coming to know ourselves as creatures of God. Teresa calls us to remember ourselves as castles made of diamond, and to enter into the reality of ourselves as treasure. "The gate of entry to this castle," she writes, "is prayer and reflection" (I:1:7).

However, stilling the soul and entering prayerfully into oneself, when one is unaccustomed to doing so, is at times a difficult, even strenuous exercise. We are accustomed to relating to ourselves and others more superficially, to busying ourselves with treading water. Being alone with our deepest selves might require grappling with deeper emotions and the soulful messages they might carry. Before we begin, we cannot know what the silences inside us will tell us. Our fears can keep us from moving more deeply into the richness of our interior lives. What if, as we begin to listen, we discover disturbing things about ourselves, things we have denied in order to cope more successfully with life? Or what if, as we listen more intently, we discover there really is nothing there? Breaking through such self-limiting fears is, for Teresa, all a part of the process of coming to true self-knowledge, an understanding of the self and its capacity in God. Apart from its created capacity, she says, the human person can be fainthearted, cowardly, even overcome by misery (see I:2:8, 10). But in its created potential each soul is truly majestic. Entering into its depths, with genuine dedication to prayer, the soul is sure to discover and manifest this truth about itself.

If, in the first dwelling places, with their metaphorical glimpses of the possibilities of the human person, we capture only that the *Interior Castle* is an itinerary toward a way of life, a way of being a person, and a way of seeing, knowing, and sharing life with God, we have already received a profound insight: that the journey toward self-knowledge and authenticity/agency as a human person is not simply a psychological project but also an ethical one, a spiritual one, and a theological one. Indeed, these apparently singular pursuits are united in and through the medium of the self, so that what is learned in any of those arenas has profound implications for the others. What is being proposed is that to construct the self is to participate in divine creativity—to enable God to come alive in one's own personhood. Composing a life, then, allows for the unfolding of the divine–human partnership, revealing what co-creation can accomplish, both in the depths of the human person and in the world.

The
Second
Dwelling
Places

*I*F WE CONTINUE in the discipline of coming to know ourselves, we proceed rather rapidly into the second dwelling places, where we actually begin to hear the voice of our Beloved, God, calling us gently to approach the inner center of ourselves. As Teresa describes it, "This stage pertains to those who have already begun to practice prayer and have understood how important it is not to stay in the first dwelling places....So these persons are able to hear the Lord's callings" (II:1:2). Whether these "callings" are mediated through others or through life events, or experienced as a form of "inner voice," we can understand that the soul experiences in these dwelling places a growing awareness or consciousness of the divine within the sphere of human activity.

This raising of the soul's consciousness is concurrently an awakening to the divine within the self and a process of becoming conscious and therefore becoming a subject and an agent in one's life experience. Yet knowledge of the God within oneself carries a new responsibility, one that the soul is not yet fully equipped to handle. Describing this stage Teresa writes:

> These rooms, in part, involve much more effort than do the first, even though there is not as much danger, for it now seems that souls in them recognize the dangers, and there is great hope they will enter further into the castle. I say that these rooms involve more effort because those who are in the first dwelling places are like deaf-mutes and thus the difficulty of not speaking is more easily endured by them than it is by those who hear but cannot speak. (II:1:2)

So, although the second dwelling places contain a wonderful invitation to greater spiritual progress, we encounter at the same time two challenges. First, we begin to realize that our understanding of ourselves has been partial at best and false at worst. Prayer may provide us with a different perspective on our life circumstances; when we contemplate our souls and their well-being or lack thereof, many of the behaviors, practices, or goals that previously appeared reasonable or acceptable now no longer seem appropriate. This can place us in the midst of the second dilemma, having to make difficult choices. Following the still, small voice in our own depths will certainly entail changes in our day-to-day behaviors and perhaps even significant life changes—changing jobs, giving up long-held dreams, severing relationships that become incompatible with the spiritual journey. What the soul is beginning to discover is that each and every life experience presents us with the opportunity to respond concretely to God in some way. However, it is not in the habit of seeing life this way or of making decisions with this orientation to God. Thus, a new form of self-knowledge ensues.

There are wider, social dimensions to this more conscious way of knowing. First, there is a need to explore the extent to which the socially defined self finds itself at odds with the self that emerges out of the knowledge of God within. Second, there is an awakened awareness of the possibility of God's presence in all daily activity; this places in sharp relief the ways in which our social patterns deny or preclude the possibility of that presence. Therefore, by definition, growth in self-knowledge entails consideration of the self beyond one's own individuality. As the soul experiences a growing consciousness of how deeply interconnected humanity is, it must also reflect on its corroboration in social, economic, political, and even religious systems that oppress and stifle human potential writ large.

In the second dwelling places, the soul hears the call of God to a deeper, more godly way of life, and the soul desires to be good—to heed and respond to this call. But, as it realizes repeatedly that it is unable to do so, it can feel crushed with shame. This is a humbling kind of self-knowledge, at times painful to the soul, as it crashes against its own limitations. Accustomed to autonomy and a reasonable amount of success in life, now the human person realizes that it is not, and cannot be, in control of its own soulful destiny. Here the soul learns its own radical need for grace, not as a foreign force, but as an orientation to goodness that works through and with us, awakened by the voice of God deep within.

> So these persons are able to hear the Lord's callings…[and] this Lord desires intensely that we love Him and seek His company, so much so that from time to time He calls us to draw near Him. And His voice is so sweet the poor soul dissolves at not doing immediately what he commands. Thus, as I say, hearing His voice is a greater trial than not hearing it. (II:1:2)

If in the first dwelling places we became aware of our great capacity, in the second dwelling places we perceive how far we are from reaching that capacity and how much effort it will take to realize that capacity.

Seeing our own shortcomings—how we are so easily overcome by "poisonous creatures"[1]—has the capacity to overwhelm and discourage us, and Teresa describes the soul in these dwelling places as "afflicted," not knowing whether to continue on its journey or turn back to the previous dwelling places, where ignorance made life easier. What carries the day in this conflict is the constancy of God's presence, which begins to instill greater power in the human will, as she writes:

> The will is inclined to love after seeing such countless signs of love; it would want to repay something; it especially keeps in mind how this true Lover never leaves it, accompanying it and giving it life and being. Then the intellect helps it realize that it couldn't find a better friend, even were it to live for many years; that the whole world is filled with falsehood; and that so too these joys the devil gives it are filled with trials, cares, and contradictions. (II:1:4)

Teresa also recommends that we seek out those with greater experience, who have dedicated themselves to the spiritual journey and who can advise us along the way. Companionship and solidarity with others can strengthen our determination to move forward in the recovery of our soulful nature.[2] At this stage, she says, we often experience God through intermediaries, or "through words spoken by other good people, or through sermons, or through what is read in good books, or through the many things that are heard and by which God calls, or through illnesses and trials, or also through a truth that He teaches during the brief moments we spend in prayer" (II:1:3). With practice it becomes easier to recognize God's voice through those intermediaries, in a process of discernment that guides the soul even as it calls it.

What is important at this stage is balance, because discouragement and even abandonment of prayer would be easy responses to the challenges posed. Such balance and perspective are gained through conversations with those who have gone through this stage and passed beyond it. They can help provide us with reassurances, compassionate concern, and guidance. Hopefully, we have learned the value—indeed, spiritual necessity—of self-care. But even once that step is accomplished, perhaps we still sometimes struggle with the idea that it is selfish to care for ourselves, and that we ought to be selfless. The truth actually lies in the proper centering of selfhood: when we care for the God in ourselves, we can also care for the God in others. Unless we take care of the God in ourselves, we will lose sight of the God all around us. And as we take care of this God, within and without, we become an integral part of the ongoing process of incarnation, God being made human.

What should be clear here is that soulful self-knowledge is not possible in a vacuum. The only way to start exploring the depths of our essential personhood is through prayer, and this includes prayerful conversations with others. We enter into prayer through quiet moments alone, reflective spaces, journal times, and conversations. The soul must begin, in order to know itself, to move outside of itself in prayer and also within itself in prayer. It is only then that it will begin to know its own breadth. Direction, mentoring, and adequate time for reflection and meditation within a safe community of similarly dedicated people are all important for the journey ahead.[3]

Teresa's insights about the soul contain a powerful cultural critique for her day and for our own. Mindfulness, deliberation, wisdom—are these values of our culture? Does not nearly everything we learn—certainly in the media, but also often in the workplace, the schools, the home, and the family—militate against them? To do things quickly, to be more efficient, to acquire more, to achieve success, even sometimes what appear to be noble desires to please others or to do good—can stand in the way of aligning our life journeys with the still, small voice inside calling us to our deepest authenticity, to being who we were created to be. We are fragile enough in this journey and need companions to help us in our daily struggles.

We also begin at this stage a process of increasing our determination to prioritize our life in God that will culminate in what Teresa calls a union of wills. Although she speaks of us as needing to "conform" ourselves to God's will, this is, as the soul comes to see later, more a question of discovering its deepest desires implanted in it by God and becoming focused on the pursuit of them, than it is the annihilation of one's personal will before an abstract, demanding God outside of the person himself or herself. While she argues that "in perfect conformity to God's will lies all our good," part of the soul's journey is to learn to trust that one's gifts as a person, strengths and weaknesses, dreams and desires are all bestowed upon one by God. Life in God, then, consists in realizing one's true potential, and realizing one's true potential is not possible outside of a conscious, willful relationship with the One who created us. There is pain in discovering that we have made life choices that have brought us into conflict with our own potential as persons. Few people have the inherent or acquired self-knowledge at early stages of their lives to recognize their own deepest potential; but the experience of the second dwelling places increasingly calls us into a greater knowledge of who we were meant to be and a greater desire to become that person.

The
Third
Dwelling
Places

*E*NTRY INTO THE THIRD dwelling places symbolizes something of a moral victory for the soul, as its dedication to prayer has led it to a state in which it is less inclined to thoughtless behavior and what Teresa calls "occasions of sin." The increased recognition of God in all things—enabled by dedication to prayer and deeper self-knowledge—allows for souls at this stage to resolve some of the more difficult questions of conscience that troubled them in the second dwelling places. Thus, Teresa writes, "Poisonous creatures rarely enter these dwelling places. If they enter they do no harm; rather, they are the occasion of gain" (III:1:3). In this sense, the soul's consciousness of God has led to a greater moral consciousness, and in the third dwelling places it acquires the habit of seeing and knowing morally, a discipline of the will. More primarily, however, the soul in the third dwelling places must open[1] itself to the invitation into a relational identity that these dwelling places extends to it. Understanding itself to be in constant relationship with the divine is the critical form of self-knowledge gained in these dwelling places—not simply a deeper form of moral knowing.

The third dwelling places are recognized as a transitional stage, in which the soul is led up to the point of what is traditionally called the union of wills. Like the "eye of the needle" referred to by Christ after his encounter with the "rich young man" in Matthew 19:16–22,[2] some will pass through them and into the "supernatural" realm of human experience begun in the fourth dwelling places; others will not.[3] This stage represents either a point of entry into deeper, transformative relationship with God or the end of the road for those who equate religion with its codes, creeds, and rituals. Indeed, the choice between the two paths is epitomized, for Teresa, by the invitation extended to the rich young man, "come, follow me." In this story, a young man approaches Jesus asking what he must do to have eternal life. After Jesus tells him to keep the commandments and reviews them with him, the young man responds, "All these I have observed; what still do I lack?" Jesus responds, "If you would be perfect, go, sell what you possess and give to the poor, and you will have treasure in heaven; and come, follow me." When the young man heard this, "he went away sorrowful; for he had great possessions."[4]

In the third dwelling places, like the rich young man, the soul is invited to move beyond a servile relationship with God and into deeper partnership with God. Indeed, it is being asked to give up its previously constructed identity in exchange for a new, relational identity with God. If the soul accepts this invitation, it will then begin to explore human-divine potential (and thus have "supernatural" experiences); if it does not, it will remain in the company of the "many" virtuous souls in the world who "guard against sin, set aside periods for prayer and recollection and practice works of charity toward others." As Teresa recognizes, the third dwelling places are "certainly…a state to be desired" (III:1:5). Yet there are other, deeper states of being to be attained. As in the story of the rich young man, the soul's ultimate destiny rests in its own choice either to follow Christ and move more deeply into all that the human–divine relationship entails or to "turn away sorrowful."[5]

Layered around Teresa's consideration of the call to "follow me," is another scriptural text, "Blessed is the one who fears the Lord" (Ps 112:1), which Teresa uses to suggest that the increased awareness of God's presence cultivated in the previous dwelling places enables us to realize that we do nothing outside the presence of God. Such knowledge of God calls us to deeper moral and spiritual accountability, not so much out of fear of damnation as out of heightened awareness of God's immanence. By "fears" Teresa means less the adoption of an attitude of servility and more an acknowledgement of God's greatness; she is calling us to revere God and recognize God's presence in all of our daily activity. The soul in the third dwelling places has an increased consciousness of the ubiquity of God, and, if it can respond with awe, reverence, and openness to the mystery of God that is being more fully revealed to it, it stands at the threshold of authentic relationship with God.

Once the soul "fears" or reveres God, it becomes determined to honor that presence in daily life, and that determination is actually a setting of the will to do the will of God, which it understands as love, growth, and holiness. Immersing itself ever more deeply in the pursuit of expressing love, it begins to remove all the impediments to truly loving. These impediments are many and varied and can be deeply embedded in the soul. It may take the soul a long time to recognize (and remove) them all. Classically, this stage is referred to as "purgation," a purging of all impediments to true union with God, a burning away of deadwood, or, to use Teresa's earlier metaphor, a thorough pruning of all the weeds that inhibit the growth of the garden of our soul.

Perhaps because Teresa had already dedicated a significant portion of the *Book of Her Life* to the metaphor of the soul as garden, she does not devote much time, in the *Interior Castle,* to the theory and practice of purgation. But in the *Life* she presents the task of the spiritual life in the following terms: "The one who is beginning [to pray] must remember that she is beginning to make a garden in very inhospitable soil, which is overrun with weeds, and must plant good ones in their stead" (*Life* 11:6).[6] Then she details the ways in which we can cultivate the garden of the soul by ensuring that it is constantly watered. In the third dwelling places we are being asked to embrace the care of our souls, not simply by ridding ourselves of the classic "vices" (habits and behaviors that keep us from full partnership with God) but also, and more fundamentally, by allowing our relationship with God to define the self.

Thus, if we place ourselves back in the position of the rich young man, we see that what Christ is asking is deeper even than the wealth or social identity of the human person. Christ is asking if we are willing to forgo the forging of our own identity as an individual and enter into a partnership where the self is not entirely autonomous. As in any true partnership, the identity of the self is enhanced, not merely limited or bound, in this relational identity. But this benefit is less obvious to the rich young man who has much at stake; indeed, what he perceives to be a loss of self-determination and autonomy is a significant deterrent for him. The soul cannot, however, enter into its relational potential without committing itself, actively through the will, to the relationship itself, as Teresa explains,

> [T]here is need of still more in order that the soul possess the Lord completely, it is not enough to say we want it, just as this was not enough for the young man whom the Lord told what one must do in order to be perfect. (III:1:6)

Again, however, it is important to point out that the union of wills is just that: a *union* of wills, not an obliteration of the human will. Teresa uses language not of self-annihilation but of actively placing the will in the service of relationality, with all of the give-and-take that relationality involves. In other words, the soul finds its identity within its relationship with God; it shares its self-determination with God and, ultimately, the soul's assent to deepen its relationship with God enables further divine–human collaboration.[7]

What becomes apparent in the narrative of the rich young man is the idea that virtue is only the beginning of life in God; the pursuit of goodness must be rooted in loving intention, so *the commitment to love* makes possible a deeper conversion into a mystical, transformative relationship with God.[8] The invitation to "come, follow me" is the invitation to begin the work of moving into a shared identity with God. Here religiosity itself deepens, and creeds and codes are lived out of love, not merely obligation. The shift in this stage—that is, what determines whether or not we will move into the ones to come—is our openness to the awakening brought about within us as we let God become an active, loving subject in our lives, on God's own terms, not our own.

For Teresa, this means accepting God as our life companion, responding to the divine presence with loving care, wherever that takes us. This habit can be inculcated within the soul through prayer, as the Jesuit tradition, an important early influence on Teresa's prayer life, teaches. It is a basic form of living in the company of Jesus through discernment, a process of meditational exercises designed to bring about knowledge of the companionate presence of Jesus, which then informs each choice a person makes in their lives. Such an approach to life will, of necessity, entail great change for the soul. But without change, at this stage, no further spiritual growth is possible, and the third dwelling places become a kind of final resting place.

Thus, the third dwelling places represent the place where we make a critical life decision, which revolves around a simple yet profound question: if we have been attentive to the loving voice we have been hearing in prayer, are we now willing to allow that voice to steer the course of our lives? To make such a choice may not seem completely reasonable, especially according to the values we have inherited from our culture. But the prioritization of "unreasonable choices" on the basis of love, compassion, and desire—the setting aside, for example, of several years of professional opportunities in order to care for a loved one who needs special attention—is a perfectly comprehensible, deeply human response: it is the movement of ethical principles into concrete, loving action, so that devotion, to God and others, is not simply theory but a way of putting love and values into practice.

Although Teresa has not yet used nuptial imagery, it is already implicit. The relationship with God is one of two who deeply long for one another, and this contributes to the dimension of "fear," for the soul is being asked to enter intimately into what it subconsciously understands to be a transformative relationship, the realms and consequences of which it cannot completely fathom. The union of wills here is not simply, then, about aligning one's will with some set of principles, or even with what one discerns to be the will of God in a particular circumstance. Rather, moving through this stage entails the kind of conscious choices one makes in a committed, loving relationship with a life partner, actively striving toward realization of one's own and the other's fullness of being, in order to share the best of self with another. Reverence and love for the Other pulls the soul out of egocentricity, calling it into deeper relationship with God, with others, and even with itself. Cultivating loving-kindness is an important first step in this process. With its growing commitment to more active forms of love, the soul is introduced into greater insight into its relational nature, seeing that its being is wrapped in the fabric of all being. If it enters into such a deepened relationship with God, it will see how intimately interwoven with God it already is, and it will not be able to live in the same ways it has before.

If God is love, then aligning one's will with that of God entails making daily, conscious choices to love and to act out of love. Here we must speak of love as not a feeling but a choice or decision to act lovingly, and Paul's classic description of love in 1 Corinthians 13 can guide those actions: we give up pride, boasting, jealousy, gloating, anger, and brooding over old wounds, and instead we devote ourselves to patience, forbearance, and kindness, rejoicing in the good and focusing on hope.[9] Acting in love also entails searching for and discovering joy in doing these things, not simply doing them out of duty, even though at times we might have to exert force initially in changing our mind-set. Love must be given freely; the spontaneity and joy of love stand in stark contrast to the actions of those who play the martyr, perfunctorily performing duties as if they will be rewarded someday and then becoming angry or self-righteous when no reward is forthcoming. Thus, the love to which we aspire is unconditional, with no expectation of return. This attitude of generosity is what we are called to cultivate as we move through the third dwelling places.[10]

Here, too, our duty is not so much what we do, but rather our duty is to work at aligning our whole selves—action, intention, and desire —with our hearts, minds, and souls, so that what we do reflects who we truly are deep inside. In practice, this means to put our loving selves into our actions and then step back gracefully to see what happens next. This, of course, is how God loves, out of God's own being, so that what God does is who God is. And we can approximate that way of being/doing when we love, if we put our whole selves into loving.

We may well have to learn and/or relearn how to love that way, for life has a way of teaching us caution in love. But children intuitively love that way, with a joy and spontaneity and fullness that so often pull at us as parents. The encouragement of this kind of free-flowing circle of love within the family is critical to the spiritual development of the child, and, if it has been interrupted through the various forms of dysfunction within the family unit—or, worse, through neglect or outright abuse—a significant amount of healing will be necessary to move into loving fully and completely. All of us have learned experientially, usually through some painful experience of rejection or abandonment, that others do not always welcome with joy and total acceptance our loving actions; indeed, in order to survive in contexts where love does not flow freely, we have often learned to suppress our instincts to love. But in these third dwelling places we take the first step toward returning to loving fully and completely by setting our will on developing that capacity and letting go of behaviors, attitudes, and fears that keep us from a deeper kind of loving.

When Teresa describes the role of reason in this stage of spiritual development, she suggests that our intellects can themselves become impediments in our movement toward total loving. We rationalize, calculate likely response and cost, and withdraw from situations out of self-protection. Reason can aid the will in resisting the imperative to prioritize the heart. In other words, reason often facilitates our *choice* to see life experiences and relationships, especially when they disappoint us, as burdens to be complained of, intellectual problems to be solved, people to be blamed. Instead of adopting this approach, Teresa encourages us to view experiences that trigger intense emotions as opportunities to learn more about ourselves, one another, and God. When love informs our reason, we choose to empathize rather than to blame, to listen rather than to judge, to ponder rather than to dissect and analyze. Our intellectual capacity is a powerful ally then, allowing us to put our intent to grow in love for others into action.

Teresa does not discount reason here, even though she says of people in the third dwelling places, "their reason is very much in control. Love has not yet reached the point of overwhelming reason" (III:2:7). "But," she continues, "I should like us to use our reason to make ourselves dissatisfied with this way of serving God, always going step by step, for we'll never finish this journey." Our fears, doubts, and rationalizations immobilize us and keep us stationary; "we don't dare go any further—as if we could reach these [deeper] dwelling places while leaving to others the trouble of treading the path for us." So, she

exhorts, "Let's abandon our reason and our fears into God's hands...
we should care only about moving quickly so as to see this Lord"
(III:2:8). An urgency of desire enables a perspective beyond the strictly
rational, opening the way to seeing God as not only a God of rules and
commandments but of immense affection and tenderness.

As the soul increases in awe and wonder, furthermore, it begins to
experience God's presence in prayer in more profound ways than it
has been accustomed to. Such "internal favors" strengthen the soul in
its desire to embrace God out of desire, not simply duty; these favors
"come brimming over with love and fortitude by which you can journey with less labor and grow in the practice of works and virtues"
(III:2:11). So the soul begins actually to experience more joy in its life
and takes heart that it will continue to progress toward greater fulfillment. The purgative work of the earlier stages is beginning to bear
fruit in a joyful, more trusting and open response to life itself, and the
soul can experience truer freedom of spirit (III:2:4).

The
Fourth
Dwelling
Places

*T*HE FOURTH DWELLING PLACES represent the beginning of the supernatural dwelling places, the stage where the soul begins to understand, through experience, what the human person can do when enabled by God. In them, the soul receives its first direct tastes of God, which reveal in immediate, if brief, ways a previously unknown depth in its own interior. Such experiences result in a new kind of self-knowledge: the soul glimpses who it can be when capacitated by God. This is an expanded, empowered sense of personhood, in which the soul, through the grace of God, can live in its deepest, created potential, and entry into it is predicated on the movement to integrate the soul's individual faculties—the will, the intellect, and the emotions—and place them in the service of its deepening relationship with God.

Teresa begins this stage of the mystical journey with a scriptural reference from Psalm 118:32: "when you have enlarged my heart." Having the heart enlarged, expanded, dilated, or stretched is the first major step in these mystical dwelling places once the soul has assented to its relational identity with God. For if the soul is truly to know the extent of God's indwelling within it, its own sense of selfhood must expand and it must grow into its capacity to house the fullness of the divine. Given the extraordinary challenges the soul experiences in this stretching process, the experiences of the fourth dwelling places should inform any conception we have of Teresa's understanding of asceticism.[1] For Teresa, asceticism consists fundamentally in the expansion of one's affective capacity—that is, in the ability to move beyond personal self-interest and to extend oneself, through compassion and charity, toward others. All too often, asceticism has been viewed as a measure of the individual person's relationship to his or her body, or to his or her world, the renunciation of which epitomized commitment to God. Teresa encourages us to think of asceticism in more relational terms: how do we respond to the daily challenges that living in community and interconnection with others pose?[2] Her insights into the discipline of love should be considered her primary contribution to the larger definition of Christian asceticism.

Thus, to put a very complex process into simple words: once the soul has chosen to grow in love, to accept the invitation through the eye of the needle, it reaches out, through prayer, to stretch itself and to be stretched in its own capacity to love. This is a process to which both the soul and God contribute, the soul by directing itself repeatedly into the presence of God, and God by absorbing the faculties of the soul in wonder at the reality of God. The stretching process is the next stage in the metaphor of the garden as we were describing it above, for as we knead the soil of our soul, we can imagine the edges of the heart being slowly massaged, preparing us for what is to come.

In the fourth dwelling places this stretching process is possible only if our reason is involved in understanding why it is now time to aspire to a wise heart. This is the place where the desire to know—particularly the intense questioning process of reason—must be tempered by awe, resulting in the development of a patient openness to mystery. As it is led into the depths of its own heart, the soul seeks not immediate answers, but a deeper way of living in and with questions. The reverence we have cultivated in the previous stage helps us in this process. For, as Teresa declares, many of the experiences in these fourth dwelling places are "so delicate that the intellect is incapable of devising a way to explain them" (IV:1:2). Such experiences convey the soul's supernatural origins, for the soul is left knowing that it could not, on its own, invent such experiences.

In the fourth dwelling places, then, the soul learns, experientially, a more fully subjective way of being, made possible by its dedication to a more integrated, affective way of knowing. Through the experiences of prayer at this stage, the soul gains a deeper knowledge and understanding of its emotive and empathic capacities. The capacity to love serves as an ordering principle in its cognitive processing of emotions; thus rather than being feelings that might confuse or bewilder the soul, limiting its range of response to the world around it, the soul begins to learn that emotions can be a powerful vehicle for expressing compassion, empathy, and its deeper, more fully subjective presence in the lives of others. Both reason and the will are placed in the service of the greater development of the soul's affective range. Thus, in these dwelling places, the act of knowing is expanded into a holistic habit of knowing, involving both the intellect and the full range of human empathic abilities. Empowered in this process by grace through even deeper experiences of prayer, the soul begins to taste here its created capacity.

The soul's expansion is accomplished in prayer by what Teresa calls "consolations" and "spiritual delights," both of which create a space within the depths of the heart where the soul can experience and learn its emotional and affective potential and be awakened into a more profound capacity for love. In order to explain the difference between the two movements, Teresa uses the analogy of two fountains and the water troughs that fill them. The way of consolations is like a fountain whose "water comes from far away through many aqueducts and the use of much ingenuity." This ingenuity is what the soul does to encourage itself in meditative prayer and commit itself to the new vision of itself growing out of such prayer (IV:2:3). Teresa describes consolations as:

> ...those experiences we ourselves acquire through our own meditation and petitions to the Lord, those that proceed from our own nature—although God in the end does have a hand in them; for it must be understood, in whatever I say, that without God we can do nothing. (IV:1:4)

Such consolations are similar to the emotions we experience in intense but "ordinary" experiences, such as a reunion with a loved one, a life accomplishment, or a stroke of good fortune (IV:1:4). The emotional dimension of them, manifested, for example, in tears, moves the person into a deeper, soulful experience. Teresa writes: "My experience of this state (I mean of this joy and consolation that comes during meditation) is that if I began to weep over the Passion I didn't know how to stop until I got a severe headache" (IV:1:6). There is a sense in which one's own natural emotions are supplemented by some supernatural experience and move out of one's individual control. The more general consciousness of God's presence felt in the third dwelling places, which enhanced the soul's moral capacity, now enhances the soul's emotive capacity. Thus the soul's emotive life is enriched by a clearer sense of God's presence in that realm, expanding exponentially its depth of feeling. We have, by definition, a hand in these experiences of deep emotion, even though "their end is in God" (IV:1:4). Still, because God supplements our own emotions, these consolations will shatter any remnants or vestiges of a hardened heart, in order to accommodate the gradual expansion of the soul's emotive and affective capacity.

At first, the process of expanding our hearts is inherently difficult. It produces "interior trials," because we resist being stretched. At the same time that we are given a new vision of ourselves through the consolations of prayer, we are also asked to move beyond controlling our own subjective, emotional state. This can be frightening and dis-orienting, particularly as we know that the experiences we are having are beyond our previous emotional "norms." The soul is disoriented by such strong feelings and experiences, distressed by "melancholy and loss of health," and may even consider abandoning prayer com-pletely (IV:1:9). It is challenged by a certain internal instability induced by the intensity of its emotional life, and it is perplexed by the inability of its own intellect to settle calmly into these states of prayer. "Just as we cannot stop the movement of the heavens, but they pro-ceed in rapid motion, so neither can we stop our mind; and then the faculties of the soul go with it, and we think we are lost and have wasted the time spent before God" (IV:1:9). The soul is not accus-tomed to being incompetent; it had, in fact, achieved a rather large accomplishment by entering the third dwelling places when it could be satisfied by a kind of reassurance about its own moral goodness. Now, in the fourth dwelling places, it is being stretched through heightened emotional states and is frustrated by the very real chal-lenges to cultivating inner tranquility posed by this process. Teresa captures this inner turmoil in this way:

Any disquiet and war can be suffered if we find peace where we live, as I have already said. But that we desire to rest from the thousand trials there are in the world and that the Lord wants to prepare us for tranquility and that within ourselves lies the obstacle to such rest and tranquility cannot fail to be very painful and almost unbearable. (IV:1:12)

The stretching process deprives us of whatever comforts we have used in the past to insulate ourselves from the hidden depths of ourselves. In short, we are hindered by our own lack of self-knowledge, confronted with the reality that we do not know our own authentic selves. As Teresa writes, "[F]or the most part all the trials and disturbances come from our not understanding ourselves" (IV:1:9). The process of self-expansion is therefore not always a smooth one; the shocks to our consciousness experienced as we gain sight of our potentiality and see how far from it we remain, even as we strive to advance, constitute a form of purgation.

The "interior battles" Teresa describes at this stage might also be understood as a form of anxiety, produced by a tension between the desire for the comfort of the known and the now-acknowledged need to stretch into the unknown (IV:1:12). And since it is "within ourselves" that such trials lie and they are an obstacle to the rest and tranquility we desire, Teresa declares that it is painful and almost "unbearable" to be disturbed by such fears. The only real remedy to the difficulties of affective stretching is for the soul to cultivate patience and to accept that it cannot comprehend, at this point, all that is being accomplished in it. As Teresa notes with characteristic pastoral insight:

There is a more and a less to this obstacle in accordance with one's health and age. Let the poor soul suffer even though it has no fault in this; we have other faults, which makes it right for us to practice patience. (IV:1:13)

She also offers the promise that such interior struggles are a temporary state in the journey and will eventually be resolved "even in this life."[3] It is perhaps easier on the soul if it concentrates on slow and deliberate steps toward its unitive goal, trusting that the new affective knowledge of itself will compensate for the challenges. Such an approach reinforces both humility and a new kind of love of God, one that is not rooted in self-interest.

Loving God with a lack of self-interest is a profoundly important—and paradoxical—concept within Teresa's schema of spiritual growth, and it has clear parallels in the four stages of loving God proposed by Bernard of Clairvaux some four centuries earlier.[4] For both authors, loving God in a "disinterested" way—Bernard's third stage of loving God is when the soul loves God for God's sake; Teresa calls this loving God "without self-interest"—moves the soul into deeply joyful experiences of God, prefatory to forms of "rapture" that will be introduced later.[5] For Teresa, reaching deeper forms of prayer happens as the soul asks less of God. Paradoxically, God rewards the soul with greater insight and deeper joy in prayer as the soul detaches itself from any expectation or specific petition in prayer. Thus, as she describes the spiritual delights, the second form of prayer experienced in the fourth dwelling places, Teresa writes:

> You will ask me how then one can obtain them without seeking them. I answer that for the following reasons there is no better way [to receive them] than the one I mentioned, of not striving for them. First, because the initial thing necessary for such favors is to love God without self-interest. Second, because there is a slight lack of humility in thinking that for our miserable services something so great can be obtained....[W]e would be laboring in vain... [for this water] is given only to whom God wills to give it and often when the soul is least thinking of it. (IV:2:9)

Returning to the analogy of the two fountains, Teresa describes the fountain that symbolizes spiritual delights as providing water more readily, easily, and directly than the previous fountain, for the source of the water is immediate, as Teresa explains:

With this other fount, the water comes from its own source, which is God. And since His Majesty desires to do so—when He is pleased to grant some supernatural favor—He produces this delight with the greatest peace and quiet and sweetness in the very interior part of ourselves. I don't know from where or how, nor is that happiness and delight experienced as are earthly consolations in the heart. I mean there is no similarity at the beginning, for afterward the delight fills everything; this water overflows through all the dwelling places and faculties until reaching the body. That is why I said that it begins in God and ends in ourselves. For, certainly, as anyone who may have experienced it will see, the whole exterior person enjoys this spiritual delight and sweetness. (IV:2:4)

Spiritual delights, therefore, are given directly by God, denoting a grace-filled dimension or depth to the experience of prayer that the soul itself is incapable of initiating or controlling. The quality of absorption intrinsic to the experience itself makes it subjectively recognizable as supernatural, and the experience begins without any necessary relationship to external circumstances.[6]

This spiritual delight is not something that can be imagined because however diligent our efforts we cannot acquire it. The very experience of it makes us realize that it is not of the same metal as we ourselves but fashioned from the purest gold of the divine wisdom. Here, in my opinion, the faculties are not united but absorbed and looking as though in wonder at what they see. (IV:2:6)

Although the soul can do nothing to initiate the spiritual delights, it can in fact cultivate a place where such prayerful moments with God can happen. Thus, instead of seeking God in external things, the soul begins to seek God within.

[I]t is a great help to seek God within where he is found more easily and in a way more beneficial to us than when sought in creatures, as Saint Augustine says after having looked for Him in many places. (IV:3:3)[7]

And this inward searching takes the form of a "gentle drawing inward ...[like] a turtle drawing into its shell...so that the soul instead of striving to engage in discourse strives to remain attentive and aware of what the Lord is working in it" (IV:3:3–4). Developing this space of attentive silence makes possible a response to the spiritual delights that the soul will experience here. As we move from consolations to spiritual delights, we are actually creating a space for the expansion of the integrity of the self, the elements of the self that participate in the experience of God. Previously, engagement has been cognitive or of the will; here the heart, too, is moved more deeply into the presence of God.

Preparation of the space for this more complete encounter with God is the expansion of the soul. In that space, through the soul's attentive, waiting silence, is communicated the immensity of God's love, just as in intimate conversation with another. This is an immediate experience of unconditional love, which begins to flow through us according to our capacity to open ourselves up as channels of it, as Teresa writes:

> What an expansion or dilation of the soul is may be clearly understood from the example of a fount whose water doesn't overflow into a stream because the fount itself is constructed of such material that the more water there is flowing into it the larger the trough becomes. So it seems is the case with this prayer and with many other marvels that God grants to the soul, for He enables and prepares it so that it can keep everything within itself. Hence this interior sweetness and expansion can be verified in the fact that the soul is not as tied down as it was before in things pertaining to the service of God, but has much more freedom. (IV:3:9)

As we begin to feel the fullness and intensity of our direct connection to God we are to ponder, wonder, and remain in awe and gracious acceptance of this experience. To analyze it too much will cut it short through second-guessing and doubting. So here "the soul should strive to cut down the rambling of the intellect...[and] enjoy it [this recollection] without any endeavors other than some loving words" (IV:3:7). Indeed, Teresa describes the soul's most appropriate response in the following way: "Almost everything lies in finding oneself unworthy of so great a good and in being occupied with giving thanks" (IV:3:8).

As we have suggested, the process of "expanding the heart" is neither easy nor painless, although it is so positive and healing. On one level it is "natural" because it speaks to our essence, our created being; it allows us to understand and even live our life's meaning and purpose. It moves us toward greater integrity, as we have gradually shed emotions such as shame or guilt or anger, which hinder our capacity to love freely and generously. On another level, it is "supernatural," because we are being capacitated by and through experiences of God, growing in love through the apprehension of God's movement in us. To grow in this way requires an ongoing dedication to change our habits and behaviors, to expand our perspectives, and to integrate into our being and personhood each new experience of ultimate reality.

This process of human growth, in its deepest sense, is the beginning of the exploration of human potentiality, especially the capacity to love. It is possible only through the full integration of the wisdom of the heart and the dilation of its capacity to feel deeply, to experience compassion and the impulse to love and serve others as well as ourselves. The growth we experience in these realms banishes "servile fears" that might before have driven or controlled us (IV:3:9). So the soul, in this state, is no longer constrained by fear in its desire to reach out in love; instead it is "left with great confidence that it will enjoy God" (IV:3:9) and is fortified in its desire to give and receive unconditional love. What Teresa indicates here is that it would be incorrect to think of the "spiritual delights" as merely a set of experiences with no residual effect in the soul. Having known through experience the healing power of God's grace, the soul can now move toward joy and true delight in God and others.

In the fourth dwelling places we open ourselves up to God and ourselves enough to have our hearts enlarged, and in doing so a critical step toward the gradual acquisition of a relational self and the soul's subsequent expansion into its own capacity is made. Teresa actually is explicit here: the heart is expanded, but this goes beyond our emotions; by "heart" she means "another part still more interior, as from something deep. I think this must be the center of the soul" (IV:2:5). Teresa's reference to the "center of the soul" is an important recall of the primary structural image she has embedded in the work at its outset, for it is in this "center of the soul" that God resides (see I:1:3).[8] The image of the castle used in the first dwelling places suggests a majestic God seated upon a throne, and this image of God is static; it captures the dimension of God that is an unchanging essence. Yet a fully living, indwelling God is dynamic and therefore needs a wide expanse in order to engage in divine activity: to move, create, and redeem. Supernatural activity in the fourth dwelling places begins the process of actualizing the soul's created potentiality as a dynamic being, created in the image of a dynamic God. Thus, in the fourth dwelling places, the soul discovers for the first time its own "center" and participates in its expansion in order to take in and move into the dynamism of God also embedded in its created nature. It therefore tastes, in the spiritual delights of these dwelling places, its own dynamic nature and its capacity for expansion with divine movement.

Clearly, the soul in the fourth dwelling places is introduced to a deeper self-knowledge as it experiences the dynamic activity of God within it. While it cannot initiate such activity, it can always open itself to its possibility, stretching itself to accommodate the living reality of God, especially by moving itself toward loving intention. Thus, the ideal context for the process of expanding the heart is to place ourselves in circumstances that facilitate our loving response. Here Teresa recommends: "[T]he important thing is not to think much but to love much; and so do that which best stirs you to love" (IV:1:7). Dedication to the expansion of our affective potential is the form of devotion that God desires of us, and, Teresa promises, the soul will continue to grow insofar as it perseveres in love:

We cannot know whether or not we love God, although there are strong indications for recognizing that we do love Him; but we can know whether we love our neighbor. And be certain that the more advanced you see you are in love for your neighbor the more advanced you will be in the love of God, for the love His Majesty has for us is so great that to repay us for our love of neighbor He will in a thousand ways increase the love we have for Him. I cannot doubt this. (see IV:3:8)

The
Fifth
Dwelling
Places

*T*HE EXPANSION OF THE SOUL experienced in the fourth dwelling places allows the soul, in the fifth dwelling places, to explore its own internal depth. We could perhaps say that, for the first time, the soul here experiences what it is to dwell deeply within itself, something that is now possible because it has entered a more fully subjective self-knowledge. Having engaged in that gentle "drawing inward" and having become aware of its own center, its experiences of prayer in the fifth dwelling places invite it to "settle" within itself. Here the space created in it through the process of expansion now becomes the location for a powerful form of transformation, which Teresa represents through the metaphor of the metamorphosis of a caterpillar into a butterfly.

The soul's capacity to love has been expanded in the fourth dwelling places. Now it will be asked to enter into a more particular kind of union with God, not simply the union to which, generically, all Christians are invited. In the fifth dwelling places the soul begins to experience God's love in fuller, more lavish, and more specific ways than in earlier dwelling places. If, in the fourth dwelling places, the soul experiences the healing and deeply peaceful, grace-filled dimensions of God's love, more commonly understood as God's agapic love, in the fifth dwelling places, the soul experiences the erotic dimensions of God's love, as it comes to understand that God cherishes it particularly and has chosen it for union, in the same deliberate way that spouses choose and dedicate themselves to each other.

To suggest that the soul begins to experience God in some kind of erotic way may strike readers unfamiliar with the Christian mystical tradition as peculiar. But, from as early as the third century, Christian theologians have used extensive commentaries on the Song of Songs to explain the nature and dynamics of the relationship between God and the human person as well as between God and the Christian community. Bernard McGinn observes, "Perhaps no book of the Bible was more central to medieval spirituality and mysticism or more problematic to contemporary readers than the Song of Songs,"[1] and Denys Turner, in the introduction to his study of medieval commentaries on the Song of Songs, writes, "The language of the love of God in the western Christian tradition is notably erotic."[2]

To understand how and why language about mystical union is inherently erotic, we must have an understanding of *eros* that is holistic, not asexual but not "merely" sexual. If *eros* is "the unique human energy which springs from the desire for existence with meaning, for a consciousness informed by feeling, for experience that integrates the sensual and the rational,"[3] we see that, within Teresa's schema, the soul with an expanded heart is just entering its erotic potential, for *eros* connotes "intimacy through the subjective engagement of the whole self in a relationship."[4] For many early Christian thinkers, *eros* described not only the mutual love of God and the soul but also the cosmic relation of all created being and God. Thus, *eros* is the creative, connective energy that fuels all movement in relation to God. Turner summarizes early Christian Neoplatonic thought:

> [T]hat *eros* which is the dynamic of the soul's return to God is one and the same with the erotic outflow from God which is our creation. The soul returns to God *as to* the source *from* which it flowed; and it returns *by means of* the same *eros* to which it returns.[5]

In the fifth dwelling places, Teresa begins to use nuptial images from the Song of Songs, even though, at this stage, the union with God cannot be consummated in the fullest senses. Instead, Teresa likens unitive experiences in these dwelling places to courtship, a time when brief, loving encounters with the intended provide glimpses of new life and relational identity. After such encounters the soul is left with the deep, experiential knowledge of how deeply it is cherished and desired, and the particularity of God's love for it is felt and known in a lasting way. These experiences also communicate to the soul that God truly wants to share God's being with it and that God asks the same of the soul. Through these experiences of God as *Eros*, the soul is gradually awakened into its own capacity to become an erotic being in the same sense that God is.[6]

Teresa emphasizes the particularity and uniqueness of the union that God and the soul will create by stating that to the fifth dwelling places "many are called but few are chosen" (Matt 22:14; cf. *Interior Castle* V:1:2). In these inner realms the soul experiences a powerful, more integrated form of union, qualitatively different from forms of union that it has experienced previously. As Teresa introduces this section, she signals immediately that what she is trying to describe defies words:

> O Sisters, how can I explain the riches and delights found in the fifth dwelling places? I believe it would be better not to say anything about these remaining rooms, for there is no way of learning how to speak of them; neither is the intellect capable of understanding them nor can comparisons help in explaining them; earthly things are too coarse for such a purpose. (V:1:1)

Yet with characteristic dedication to capturing the ineffable, Teresa describes what the soul experiences as a form of death to the world "so as to live more completely in God." The state of "death" is an "uprooting from the soul of all the operations the latter can have while being in the body," a suspension of normal experience "in order to dwell more perfectly in God," and it is intense enough to take away its very breath. ("If it does breathe, it is unaware that it is doing so" [V:1:3].)

One of the most distinctive features of this new form of union is how completely absorbing it is; it overcomes the soul to the point that its normal cognitive abilities are temporarily diminished. This type of union is experienced as a kind of suspension of time, as she writes: "As a matter of fact, during the time that the union lasts the soul is left as though without its senses, for it has no power to think even if it wants to" (V:1:3). The soul is temporarily united to the very essence of God, a situation that it itself cannot bring about but that is so powerful that Teresa claims, "I would dare say that if the prayer is truly union with

God the devil cannot even enter or do any damage. His Majesty is so joined and united with the essence of the soul that the devil will not dare approach, nor will he even know about this secret." Even we ourselves, with all the distractions that can engage us, cannot impede the fullness of this union (V:1:4).

Thus, union in the fifth dwelling places "is above all earthly joys, above all delights, above all consolations, and still more than that." Previous unions, she writes, were felt as if from the surface of the skin, whereas union in the fifth dwelling places is felt "in the marrow of the bones" (V:1:5). Here Teresa indicates that the soul has acquired, through ongoing meditative practice, a deeper capacity to experience God in its depths, and thus she emphasizes the *interiority* of this union. But this union is also transformative by its nature, as Denys Turner puts it, simply: "Within erotic love I am both more *me* and more *than* me."[7] The relational identity into which the soul was invited in the fourth dwelling places is now being forged within the soul's own depths, bringing about a radical transformation of its self-hood. Temporarily suspended from all normal external and internal activity while it is in these states of union, the soul is absorbed into the immediate presence of God.[8] Although the union is brief, it is intense enough to communicate to the soul immediately that it is indeed true union with God, embedding in the soul a kind of lasting wisdom about the identity of God. Teresa writes: "God so places Godself in the interior of that soul that when it returns to itself it can in no way doubt that it was in God and God was in it" (V:1:8). Indeed, for Teresa, the certainty left in the soul is one of the experiential elements of this kind of union, for "whoever does not receive this certitude does not experience union of the whole soul with God, but union of some faculty, or...one of many other kinds of favors God grants souls" (V:1:10).

After describing the subjective experience of this union, Teresa uses two metaphors to convey more fully its dynamics. First there is the scriptural metaphor of the wine cellar of Song of Songs 2:4, which we ourselves cannot enter, but into which God places us when and as God desires (V:1:11). Second, this dwelling place is also like the cocoon providing the safe space for the metamorphosis of the caterpillar, an image Teresa develops in chapter 2 of the fifth dwelling places. Embedded in this image is the "natural" process of transformation: the caterpillar, by eating mulberry leaves and spinning its own cocoon out of its mouth does what is in it to prepare itself for transformation. The cocoon is understood to be the "house" of Christ into which the soul comes to dwell, as Teresa writes: "Once this silkworm is grown... it begins to spin the silk and build the house wherein it will die. I would like to point out here that this house is Christ. Somewhere, it seems to me, I have read or heard that our life is hidden in Christ or in God (both are the same), or that our life is Christ" (V:2:4; cf. Col. 3:3–4).

The expansion of the heart or dilation of the soul accomplished in the fourth dwelling places bears fruit in the creation of an expansive space that can accommodate the transforming union with God. But in the fifth dwelling places, the soul is beginning, through the moments of unitive encounter, to share in the essence of God by participation, causing a transformation of personhood. The center of the soul where these exchanges between God and the soul occur is being made into the very dwelling place of God, and God is becoming the very dwelling place of the soul. As Teresa explains:

> His Majesty Himself, as He does in this prayer of union, becomes the dwelling place we build for ourselves. It seems I'm saying that we can build up God and take Him away since I say that He is the dwelling place and we ourselves can build it so as to place ourselves in it. And, indeed, we can! Not that we can take God away or build Him up, but we can take away from ourselves and build up, as do these little silkworms. For we will not have finished doing all that we can in this work when, to the little we do, which is nothing, God will unite Himself, with His greatness, and give it such high value that the Lord Himself will become the reward of this work. (V:2:5)

The soul cannot, on its own, control its own transformation, for the unitive states with God experienced in these dwelling places are not available on demand; however, it is important to note how Teresa uses the metaphor of metamorphosis to suggest that the ability to move from caterpillar to butterfly is embedded in the soul's very own created nature. The metaphor reinforces the need for the soul to be transformed as an integral part of its preparation for union with God, at the same time that it suggests that this transformation is not violently done to it, in opposition to its own nature, but through an organic process germane to its deepest identity. Collaboration with God in the work of transformation enables this metamorphosis to take place.

This deeper identity, as the soul emerges from the cocoon, is new, both with respect to itself and with respect to God. The butterfly represents a new, more actualized form of the individualized self as well as the emerging relational self. In this stage, the human person is now consciously theonomous, striving to name itself "with reference to its origin and destiny in God,"[9] and doubly empowered through the divine working *in* it and *with* it. Its new *relational identity*, then, represents a way of being with God, in an intersubjective relationship that it could not have supported in its previous state of selfhood. In this identity it does not cease to be itself, yet its very selfhood has been transformed as a result of its relationality. This is a realization of what Turner identifies as the foundation of mystical theology: "We begin to glimpse what union with God can mean, and equally what true human identity can be, only when the languages of both [personal identity and union] are pushed to the limit and are there *held together*."[10]

The fifth dwelling places also include the stage at which the butterfly emerges from the cocoon and now learns to live with the possibilities and challenges its new identity generates. First, of course, it is taken up with a completely new, relational self-knowledge. Teresa expresses this by writing that, as a result of its unitive experiences with God, the soul's very being has been so transformed that it "doesn't recognize itself" (V:2:6). Having been placed inside the grandeur of God, the soul finds itself now in possession of tremendous faculties to do good and to desire goodness. Thus there is a stage in these dwelling places that we might identify as "emergence," where the soul must grow into its relational nature, just as a newly emerged butterfly must allow its wings to dry and must practice flight before it can attain true mobility.

Both the metaphor of metamorphosis and the language Teresa uses to describe the soul's radically changed nature are significant enough to merit more consideration. In presenting the metaphor in all of its complexity, I have tried to highlight at once the "newness" of the butterfly's identity vis-à-vis its identity as a caterpillar, the organic process of growth that leads to this new identity, and the new relationality that fuels the soul's transformation, all of which are significant in Teresa's theological system. In presenting us with such a complex metaphor, Teresa seems to suggest an inclusive "both/and" interpretive strategy. One would be tempted, for example, to think that, since the soul cannot effect the unitive states that enable its own transformation, the soul is relatively passive in this process.[11] However, Teresa is also clear in presenting the soul as a continuing agent in the process of transformation, doing what is in it to do and opening itself relationally to allow for divine activity to operate in it what it itself cannot do.[12] As Edward Howells notes in his analysis of the fifth dwelling places, this reinforcement of the continuing activity of the human person within the dynamics of unitive activity is a theological development in Teresa's thought. In her earlier reflections on mystical union, contained in the *Life*, Teresa used language that suggested that as the soul moved toward union with God, it was completely overcome in such a way that its agency appeared diminished.[13]

But the more Teresa experienced of the mystical life and grew as a theologian, the more she saw that the mystical journey was actually the soul's growing realization, in itself, of the same kind of union of divinity and humanity that characterizes Christ. Thus, the language of transformation in the fifth dwelling places is a way of expressing how the union of divinity and humanity that characterizes Christ can also be learned, through Christ, within the human person. To understand this more clearly, we should review the christological formula enunciated at the Council of Chalcedon in 451, in which Christ was understood to be one in being with God and one in being with humanity:

truly divine and truly human, both of these in unbreakable unity. This doctrine teaches that Christ brings together in his being humanity and divinity in such a way that there is never any division between those two natures, and to think of Christ as more divine than human is erroneous. However, as Elizabeth A. Johnson so cogently reminds us, much of the Christian theological tradition had neglected to account for the implications of this understanding of Christ, one that unifies perfectly, in a "full communication of idioms," the divine and the human:

> [W]hen people, including theologians, said that Jesus had two natures, they implicitly thought of each of these natures as comprising one-half the total picture. Jesus became so to speak, 50/50, partly divine and partly human, or totally divine and partly human, but not truly divine and truly human, 100/100 as Chalcedon had confessed.[14]

In Christ humanity and divinity are shown to be complementary at the same time that their fullness is revealed, so that at the same time that the fullness of God's divinity is revealed in Christ, so, too, humanity is brought into its own fullness. Christ then makes real, visible, and incarnationally experienceable the fullness of humanity, not only the fullness of divinity; both fullnesses are known simultaneously through Christ. In Christ, a new kind of human-divine agency is learned, one in which humanity, united with divinity, both comes into its own fullness and is united with something beyond itself. Using this language enables us to see how Christ, then, in and through the fullness of humanity and divinity, enables humanity's erotic potential, and this is precisely what the soul in the fifth dwelling places begins to see, from its new vantage point as "butterfly."

Thus, what Teresa suggests is that in the fifth dwelling places, the soul learns a new form of divine-human agency, predicated upon its new life in Christ, a life that the soul, by itself, cannot sustain. As Howells points out, this "true union" is stronger and has deeper ontological implications than the "delightful union" of the fourth dwelling places. As he puts it, in the fifth dwelling places, "the soul becomes Christ in its humanity by working to die with Christ, and to this God unites himself, just as God and humanity are united in Christ."[15] This "true union" is experienced deeply but only briefly, so that, at the level of the fifth dwelling places, a great perspectival difference arises for the soul. In its transformed state, it now has the capacity to see reality from a divinely informed perspective. This form of sight, or insight, provides a vista into whole new realms of possibility in the world, inspiring it to much greater and engaged activity. Like Christ, the soul seeks to convey the magnitude of God's love to others, and this desire sparks creative, redemptive, and charitable works. By itself, however, the soul cannot translate this desire into action. Indeed, a full partnership of humanity and divinity will require a great deal of dedication and ongoing grace. Thus, through both continuing habit and the operation of grace, the soul realizes in itself, just as Christ did, what we could call the fullness of incarnational potentiality.

At the level of the fifth dwelling places, however, the soul only glimpses the potentiality of divine–human union, coming to know it slowly, just as in betrothal what is known is not simply who the intended spouse is but what the potential of the union between self and intended holds. On a practical level, however, the soul recognizes its ongoing limitations as an individualized self. In its unitive moments it has one perspective; in its more "ordinary" moments it has another. This perspectival difference, which we will examine below, translates, in action, into a kind of restlessness and self-dissatisfaction; just as the butterfly cannot soar immediately, the soul cannot accomplish its own aspirations toward goodness. Born of relational encounters, the soul's desire to make God's presence more manifest in the world also depends on relational activity, and the soul is not yet fully in possession of its relational identity. The soul's new "wings" give it both a new, much broader view of the world and more insight into the possibilities of life in God: a new potential, new insights, a new consciousness have been born in it. Its desire to teach and spread the knowledge of these possibilities overwhelms it. Further, it has experienced deep peace and rest in the unitive experiences of God, which it cannot replicate. As Teresa describes the soul here, "it doesn't know where to alight and rest. Since it has experienced such wonderful rest, all that it sees on earth displeases it, especially if God gives it this wine often. Almost each time it gains new treasures" (V:2:8). The soul seeks conversational companionship with other humans, but many times even that is denied it, for often its ordinary companions have not had similar transformative experiences. Indeed, their struggle to comprehend the soul's changed state may present new relational challenges.

The soul must radically reorient itself to accommodate and develop its new reality.

> It no longer has any esteem for the works it did while a worm, which was to weave the cocoon little by little; it now has wings. How can it be happy walking step by step when it can fly? On account of its desires, everything it can do for God becomes little in its own eyes. (V:2:8)

Here Teresa highlights the dilemma of the soul at this stage in its development: its desire for human-divine activity has been ignited by its initial entry into a new state of being. Yet it cannot bring about the unitive experiences that both orient it to that level of activity and enable it to participate in such activity. The soul's movement into a new sphere of divine-human potentiality both empowers the soul and leaves it terribly vulnerable; its subjective state is now more than ever conditioned by relationality, an intersubjective way of being that the individual self cannot control. This kind of vulnerability, while difficult to sustain, is critical to acquiring deeper compassion and solidarity with God and others.[16]

As the soul examines the world from this new relational perspective, it suffers from "seeing God offended" (V:2:14), and it has a deep desire "to save souls" (V:2:13). These passions run very deep within the soul—they are felt in "the intimate depths of our being" and the pain of evils suffered and inflicted in the world, crimes against God, "breaks and grinds the soul into pieces" (V:2:11). This suffering is a participation in human suffering at large, a realization that human cruelty is an expression of the terrible falsity that God is not somehow an integral part of the human story. Any rejection of the presence of God in an individual human person or in humanity at large cannot help but affect this soul deeply.

Experiences of the soul's new relational perspective highlight for us that the soul in the fifth dwelling places must negotiate between two states of being and suffers with the lack of integration of these two states. Indeed, in the sixth dwelling places, the soul's experience of the difference between these two states of being only intensifies, causing the gradual disintegration of its own being as a self outside of God.[17]

One of the ways that Teresa characterizes this process, as she looks back at it from the perspective of the seventh dwelling places, is:

> [I]t seemed to her that there was, in a certain way, a division in her soul. And while suffering some great trials a little after God granted her this favor [i.e., of God's company], she complained of that part of the soul, as Martha complained of Mary, and sometimes pointed out that it was there always enjoying that quietude at its own pleasure while leaving her in the midst of so many trials and occupations that she could not keep it company. (VII:1:10)[18]

This passage appears to reflect the great differences the soul experiences when it feels divine accompaniment and when it does not. In its unitive moments, it experiences a relational subjectivity that is distinctly at odds with the subjectivity it feels as an individual entity. The soul's self-perception—and perhaps its experiential reality—is one of division.[19]

As the soul becomes increasingly exposed to the reality of God, it finds the denial of God in any context very painful. Having experienced God so directly and tangibly, it increasingly wants to be an instrument or agent in manifesting God's presence in the world and indicating it to others who do not recognize it. But, as it is not yet habituated to discovering or manifesting the presence of God in all things, experiences of painful absence reinforce for it what it continues to lack in itself.[20] It does not yet know how to affirm the essential presence of God in all things in such a way that will transform systemic denials of God's presence in the world. Its heightened vulnerability in this regard necessitates strong companions in its spiritual journey, for perhaps humans cannot sustain the realization of the God-human potential without tender, ongoing support mediated by other humans.

As the soul is increasingly sensitized to the presence of God and concurrently distressed by the many ways that humanity fails to recognize or even outright denies that presence, it experiences many forms of discouragement. With time, however, the soul learns that it contains within itself the remedy to its own suffering, for it can always manifest God's presence through loving actions. Thus Teresa encourages, "The Lord asks of us only two things: love of God and love of our neighbor. These are what we must work for. By keeping them with perfection, we do God's will and so will be united with God" (V:3:7). Although love of neighbor may tax us at times, when rooted in love of God, such love becomes easier, and the ascetical discipline of love is the greatest indicator of our desire to please and do the will of God. Teresa advises:

> When you see yourselves lacking in this love [i.e., perfect love of neighbor], even though you have devotion and gratifying experiences that make you think you have reached this stage, and you experience some little suspension in the prayer of quiet (for to some it then appears that everything has been accomplished), believe me, you have not reached union. And beg our Lord to give you this perfect love of neighbor. Let His Majesty have a free hand, for He will give you more than you know how to desire because you are striving and making every effort to do what you can about this love. (V:3:12)

Aspiring to this kind of love, and being enabled in this kind of love by God, is the "ordering of charity" that occurs in the bride taken into the wine cellar in the Song of Songs,[21] and it prepares the soul for the spiritual betrothal with God that will occur in the sixth dwelling places.

In the fifth dwelling places we learn experientially the particularity and depth of God's love through a new knowledge of God as *Eros*; we are transformed by this knowledge; and we endeavor to commit to sharing this love with others. Both our capacities and our responsibilities as loving beings are enhanced here, through glimpses of what is already happening in us through our erotic relationship with God. Moved by the vision of our deepest identity as a human person capacitated in God, we seek deeper erotic union with God, and we commit ourselves to all that such a relationship will involve. Teresa concludes the fifth dwelling places by encouraging us to strive always to advance, for, she writes, "love is never idle, and…a soul that has tried to be the betrothed of God, that is now intimate with His Majesty, and has reached the boundaries that were mentioned must not go to sleep" (V:4:10).

The
Sixth
Dwelling
Places

*T*HE SIXTH DWELLING PLACES are the most comprehensive, experientially dense, and theologically difficult section of the mystical journey and of the text of the *Interior Castle* itself. None of the material contained in these dwelling places is superfluous, although it is difficult at first to see how it fits together to form a unified whole. Few scholars have given the theological content of the sixth dwelling places much attention, and those who have tend to conclude something similar to Rowan Williams, who writes: "It is hard to see completely clearly what is distinctive in this phase: that is, what is *theologically* distinctive over and above an intensification of peculiar phenomena."[1] To arrive at the theological content of the sixth dwelling places, we will have to explore what the soul's deepening encounters with God are actually accomplishing within it: the slow (indeed, at times, difficult and even painful) realization of a new form of theonomous personhood. For if theonomy is the naming of the human person with reference to its origin and destiny in God, the sixth dwelling places constitute God's deeper invitation into the reality of an identity shaped by the union of human and divine as modeled by Christ.

Because Teresa describes so many different types of visionary and ecstatic experiences in the sixth dwelling places, it is easy for the reader to get caught up at that level of the text. Exhaustive descriptions of what are called "paramystical phenomena" suggest that Teresa intended the sixth dwelling places to serve as a manual for the discernment of spirits, much needed by women in the 1570s, given the suspicion of both mental prayer and embodied religious experience. But there is a great deal more being conveyed in this material. Hidden underneath all the explanatory detail is the chronicle of a gradual appropriation of a new relational identity, a deeper form of personhood rooted in actual ontological transformation but predicated, too, upon a deepening consciousness of and sensitivity to the reality of

God. In this sense, we can see that the soul's deepening awareness of theological reality (God's reality, as God gradually reveals this reality to the soul in these dwelling places) is an epistemological journey with ontological effects entailing a shift in both *what* and *how* the soul knows. We can retrieve an outline of this process by examining the effects on the soul of the many unitive experiences and how they are related both to the soul's ongoing transformation and to the intensification of its relational identity. This outline will, in turn, give us a clearer sense of the critical shift in the human–divine relationship realized in these dwelling places.

In his insightful description of Teresa's understanding of experience, Edward Howells provides a clearer framework for exploring our theological understanding of the sixth dwelling places. As Howells notes, Teresa has a complex definition of "experience," by which "she does not mean sensations or emotions but a field of knowledge, which in mystical union is the field of supernatural or immediate knowledge of God....Experience is the skill brought by one who knows not just something *about* the object under view but how to orient and position itself in *relation* to this object in order to grasp it accurately."[2] But as the soul increasingly comes to know itself and God as subject, experience takes on even deeper meanings, as Howells begins to suggest when he writes that "experience is gradually transformed from the natural way of knowing to the mystical way of knowing God." By the sixth dwelling places, then, we can say that the experience is the further "'expansion' of the soul as the soul comes to know God mystically."[3] Finally, Howells argues, experience is "at root, a dynamic relational ability, a self-other relation, which is expanded by mystical transformation," so that it has as its ultimate goal "an inner-trinitarian, intersubjective union with God."[4] Thus Teresa's descriptions of "experiences," when viewed in their aggregate, paint a composite portrait of the *process* of union with God, showing how, as the soul develops its relational potential, it learns and takes into itself its shared identity with the trinitarian God.[5]

In the sixth dwelling places, then, the soul is assimilating or apprehending a unitive identity, an identity made possible only in and through God: the perfection of human personhood in the image and likeness of God. This process epitomizes the definition of *theōsis* proposed by Catherine Mowry LaCugna, who writes: "The ultimate good of human beings is to achieve *theosis*, to realize the fullness of our humanity in union with the Trinity."[6] Because God's identity is trinitarian, the soul takes in the very being of God, a God who *is* and is *known in* loving relationality. Thus, the God increasingly known in the sixth dwelling places is not static, and, as the soul is united with God, it takes into itself, through unitive movements, the dynamism that characterizes God's being.

By definition, then, the union being forged is one of mutual, complementary partnership. It is a partnership enabled by God, through the transformative process whose elements are described in the sixth dwelling places. Here, the natural/supernatural distinction is being blurred; the edges and points of the soul's boundaries being rubbed smooth, so that it adopts a fluidity or malleability that replicates the flow of energy among the persons of the Trinity. An intensification of supernatural activity within the soul accomplishes this transformation, but the soul always participates in this process, even though it entails visions, locutions, raptures, and other embodied and perceptual experiences that the soul can neither initiate nor control. Because the soul experiences both a heightened subjectivity and a loss of autonomous agency, the temptation, in interpreting this material, has been to conclude that the soul loses itself in some form of self-annihilation. But such an interpretation goes directly against what Teresa has revealed to us at the outset of the journey: the soul's majesty consists of the reality that it is created in the image and likeness of God. In the sixth dwelling places, the soul begins to move definitively into this, its own deepest reality. Another conclusion, drawn by Rowan Williams, that in the sixth dwelling places the human–divine relation becomes fully established in its direction toward God and "some kind of decisive surrender has been made, the surrender without which final union would not be possible,"[7] needs further exploration.

Although the sixth dwelling places depict the intensification of the soul's experience of the Otherness of God deep within its own interior, I would suggest that the soul learns, experientially, not "surrender" to its dynamics but increased "movement" with them. And the kind of movement the soul learns is none other than *perichōrēsis*, the word used "to highlight the dynamic and vital character of each divine person, as well as the coinherence and immanence of each divine person in the other two."[8] *Perichōrēsis*, sometimes translated as "the divine dance," a "being-in-one-another," a "permeation without confusion,"[9] is the very movement of God, the movement that characterizes the relationality of the persons of the Trinity and that allows for intersubjective union with God.[10]

If the movement of God is erotic in nature, as we began to argue in our analysis of the fifth dwelling places,[11] then the soul begins to learn experientially a "primordial truth" captured by some of Teresa's predecessors in the Christian mystical tradition: "Creation itself is an explosion of erotic energy, the ecstasy of a God who, in his act of creating, stands outside himself, perhaps literally 'beside himself' with love." Consequently, "if the created order, and if we ourselves, are the ecstatic outflow of God, then our return to God is our reciprocating ecstasy, our standing outside ourselves in God."[12] In the fifth dwelling places, the soul was awakened into its own erotic potential so that now, in the sixth dwelling places, through increasing unitive encounters with God, it can learn gradually how to share in God's erotic activity.

Before we proceed to explore the multiple steps in this learning process, it is important to clarify two points: first, the idea that, in God, *agapē* and *eros* are interchangeable, and its corollary, that the erotic relationship between God and humanity is one of mutuality, if not of equals. On the first point, we note that early Christian thinkers who explored commonalities between Greek philosophical systems and Hebrew and Christian scripture often concluded that "the sacred writers regard 'yearning' (*eros*) and 'love' (*agape*) as having one and the same meaning."[13] The fundamental insight of these thinkers, one that is often lost to us today,[14] is that, in God, there is an essential unity of all loving activity, a passionate expression of ultimate care that humans can learn and perhaps even assimilate. Thus, loving activity in God represents a superabundant fullness of divinity; spilling out of itself, its actions create, sustain, and draw humanity into its own fullness, a "100%" fullness, of the type realized in the person of Christ, as Elizabeth Johnson has argued.

The abundance of material in the sixth dwelling places describing ways that the soul is touched by God, then, is meant to characterize the radical ontological shifts that take place within the soul, as it learns not merely to accommodate divine presence and activity but to integrate it fully into the depths of its being. As it does so, of course, it concurrently understands that this presence is not merely foreign to it, taken in during momentary encounters with the divine, but is also a heretofore unrealized part of its own nature.[15] Together, then, the soul and God begin, at this stage, to make incarnately real the created capacity of the soul. Theologically, this process can be best expressed as the disintegration of forms of personhood rooted in anything less than humanity's created potential and the concurrent reintegration of personhood into human form created "in the image of God" (see Gen 1:26). Such a model is more helpful and more consistent with the mutuality suggested by nuptial imagery than the more traditional model of surrender and "being overcome" by God.[16] For, as Denys Turner observes:

> To love erotically is to yearn for an identity of lover with the beloved which surpasses that which can be attained within any other kind of relationship between them....The search for erotic mutuality is the search for a union that does not conflict with differentiation and for a differentiation which is not set at odds with union; and so it is at least implicitly the yearning for a condition in which the very contrast between union and differentiation is itself transcended, a condition in which the affirmation of the one is not bought at the price of the denial of the other.[17]

Some of these interpretive difficulties are raised by the metaphor Teresa uses to characterize the sixth dwelling places: at the outset of this section, she tells us that the sixth dwelling places are the place "where the soul is now wounded with love for its Spouse" (VI:1:1). This "wound of love" is traditional language to describe the state of heightened arousal between the lovers in Song of Songs 5:8, alternately translated: "I adjure you, O daughters of Jerusalem, if you find my beloved, that you tell him I am sick with love" (RSV). Origen in his *Commentary on the Song of Songs*, equates this "wound of love" with "being smitten through with the dart of God's passionate love [*eros*]."[18] Throughout the medieval period, later mystics used the metaphor of "wound" to represent and explore the point of entry into deeper connection with divinity, particularly as an avenue into union with Christ through the wounds or opening in his own body.[19] Teresa's use of the wound of love is, in fact, quite consistent with its introduction toward the end of the Song of Songs, when the lovers have established a confidence in one another's love and fidelity and express their connected identity ("My beloved is mine and I am his" [2:16]). In Teresa's model, the soul receives the wound of love in the sixth dwelling places, once it has already increased in self-knowledge and has focused its will and its desires on union with God.

Thus, for Teresa, the "wound of love" is the opening created in the soul for God's communication of the erotic reality of human–divine interaction. Unitive experiences in the sixth dwelling places serve both to intensify the soul's desire for God and to convey experientially the new potentiality that unitive activity with God generates within the soul. The paradigm that Teresa explores is how the fullness of union with God endows the soul with strength; over the course of repeated experiences of such union, the soul comes into its deepest potentiality, which is not of its own nature as an individual, but *is* within its growing nature as a partner of God; this is its potentiality-in-God, as she writes: "From this union comes its fortitude" (VI:1:2).

As the point of entry into deeper union with God, the "wound" represents both gain and loss to the soul; it gains increased relational identity and new potentiality, while it loses a selfhood predicated on individual identity and autonomy. If we recall that the soul has been developing its affective capacities through the fourth and fifth dwelling places, we note that by the time it has reached the sixth dwelling places it is intensely sensitive to the effects of God's presence within it. The soul's hypersensitivity and the greater depth of human–divine encounters in the sixth dwelling places leave the soul extremely vulnerable to both the joy and the pain that the wound represents.[20] However, because the "wound" is also the opening for divine communication and deeper relationality, Teresa describes it as "something precious" from which the soul "would never want to be cured" (VI:2:2). It is "delightful and sweet" even as the initial pain of it "reaches to the soul's very depths" (VI:2:4). These experiences of heightened sensitivity to God's presence focus the soul's desires and orient it in an absolute way to pursue union with God as a permanent state and ultimate reality, as Teresa writes: "All these sufferings are meant to increase one's desire to enjoy the Spouse" (VI:4:1). Thus the soul is catapulted into a new experience of profoundly "missing God," and this experience of God's absence after the radical experience of presence induces emptiness and longing powerful enough to be understood as "suffering."[21]

Teresa's reflections on entrance and absence have suggested, for some, a phallic image of God penetrating the soul,[22] but this is a facile and limited reading of the text. Encounters with God take multiple forms, often drawing the soul out of itself, releasing it from any known or previously perceived boundary of its own selfhood.[23] While both pain and joy characterize the initial wounding process, Teresa also describes other, more peaceful unitive experiences in the sixth dwelling places, encounters that do not involve pain but continue to induce delight. These encounters are more subtle, though equally intense, "as though a fragrance were suddenly to become so powerful as to spread through all the senses" (VI:2:8). Unitive experiences in the sixth dwelling places both erase and reinforce boundaries between self and Other in the same kind of linguistic dance of erotic play as in the Song of Songs. Teresa's visionary insights into the nature of God reinforce *eros* as a way of knowing God and provide readers with a broad array of images to expand our own thinking about the nature of *eros*.

In this complex tangle of experiential and expository narrative, then, Teresa appears to propose a broad and inclusive definition of ecstasy, one that places her squarely within a long tradition of mystical thought, even as she synthesizes ecstatic self-knowledge more deeply than many of her predecessors. Individual experiences of visions, locutions, rapture and ecstatic union, as Teresa describes them here, induce a great number of subjective states, no single one of which can define ecstasy. So ecstasy is not, ultimately, about fruition or the dynamics of presence and absence, although such experiences of and reflection on these kinds of experiences form a part of the process. Most fundamentally, Teresa suggests, ecstasy is about assimilating an intersubjective identity and learning to sustain intersubjectivity. Thus, at the level of experience, ecstasy expands the boundaries of the normativity of the self, dissolving perceptual and experiential limitations and enabling intersubjectivity—the ongoing process of becoming more deeply a self-in-and-with-Other/others.[24]

Thus it seems more germane to suggest that, as she describes the subjective feelings of the experiences contained in these dwelling places, Teresa's intent is to capture the variety of ways in which the boundaries of selfhood and individuality are disintegrating, and that divine *eros* is experienced here not as violent but as deeply powerful in the eradication of such boundaries. The disintegration of the known self must, at some level, be experienced as a form of loss, and therefore would bring pain; however, to fixate on Teresa's reflection on pain at the expense of her description of other dimensions of the experience is to force a masochistic interpretation that is foreign to her thought.[25] Thus, one of Teresa's contributions in our understanding of the role of *eros* in the mystical journey is that heightened desire, stimulated by unitive encounters, keeps the soul from any residual tendency to be complacent, to leave any stone unturned in exploring its capacity for union with God.

Another important contribution is her recognition of the centrality of experience in self-knowledge, particularly in gaining a fuller comprehension of relationality. The experiences of the sixth dwelling places form another, critical stage in the soul's growth in self-knowledge, which I suggest that we consider as both revelatory self-knowledge and erotic self-knowledge. Indeed, as the soul is learning, the erotic nature of God, or what Bernard McGinn has called EROS I, makes the two terms interchangeable.[26] In its unitive encounters, the soul is taught more about itself; previously unknown aspects of its life or its nature are revealed to it by a source deeper than itself. While the soul profits tremendously from such insights, it also realizes a deeper human truth: we cannot fully know ourselves on our own; it takes relationality to move us into the fullest forms of self-knowledge and self-actualization. Thus, the revelatory, erotic self-knowledge the soul gains in these dwelling places is the comprehension of its nature as a being in relation to all being. And its unitive encounters reinforce both its relationality and its partiality as an individual. The soul acquires the subjective knowledge of its own incompletion, felt most particularly, perhaps, when the soul yearns for unitive encounters. The quality of yearning, at this stage in the soul's development, is not merely for an escape from solitude or for experiences that would draw the soul out of itself. The yearning, at once sharp and dull, is the knowledge that the wholeness the soul desires rests now, completely, in an intersubjective way of being that conditions not only its will but its desires, choices, activities, and orientations—in short, its very directionality and movement. Yet, precisely because it is an intersubjective way of being that conditions it, the soul cannot learn, on its own, the intersubjective movement that will gradually pull it into the fullness of unitive being.

There can be a deep pain caused by the consciousness of one's own incompletion, whether at the level of our human relations or in our desires to be with God in ways that we ourselves cannot attain. Teresa's traditional language of "human misery," her keen perception of her own—indeed, humanity's own—ongoing faults, failures, and shortcomings punctuates and provides counterpoint to her sense of the exquisite and inherent beauty of the unitive encounters themselves. In the sixth dwelling places the soul has a number of unitive experiences with God of various types, designed to draw it out of the confines of its own being and bring it more deeply into the subjective reality of God. These unitive experiences take the form of visions, locutions, and raptures, and each of these is explained in detail, with characteristics that will enable the reader to identify the experiences. As the *Interior Castle* is the only text in sixteenth-century Spain to present an explicit, sympathetic treatment of the subjective experience of embodied prayer, Teresa's painstaking detail in this section demonstrates two things: her radical commitment to the integrity of the mystical journey as a unifier of body and soul and deep theological insights into the loving God, concurrently incarnate and transcendent, that embodied mystical prayer reveals.[27]

In some very real ways, the material in the sixth dwelling places is a continuation of the experiences of the fifth dwelling places; yet there are some significant differences both in intensity and in direction. In the fifth dwelling places Teresa has written, "[A]lthough what is in this dwelling place and the next are almost identical, the force of the effects is very different" (V:2:7). Perhaps their most significant difference, in addition to the radical specificity of certain experiences in the sixth dwelling places, is that they are directionally different. In the fifth dwelling places the soul experiences encounters with God in its most profound center, which it comes to realize is rooted in God. It experiences the presence of God within its own soulhood, so to speak. However, in the sixth dwelling places, this process seems to turn inside-out, and the soul is drawn outside of itself in rapture. It is pulled out of its own soulhood and into the vastness of God, which it cannot tolerate except for brief periods of time. So it is returned back to itself after momentary, time-bound periods of God's infiniteness.

These repeated experiences of the presence of the vastness of God and the absence experientially of that same vastness once it has returned to the finitude of the soul as an entity still separate from God produce a profoundly disorienting experience of reality. The experience of God's awesome presence introduces the soul to a realm of ultimate reality, but because it cannot tolerate that ultimate reality in any permanent way, the soul is thrown back into its own finitude, which it then experiences as a profound lack of the ontological permanence of God. The soul is actually moving experientially somehow between time-bound reality and limitless reality. The soul becomes conscious of its own precarity outside of God, tottering with one foot in the realm of *chronos* and one in the realm of *kairos*.[28] In this sense, the soul is learning, in the sixth dwelling places, how to walk in the reality of God, so that, by the seventh dwelling places, the soul can move with grace between the two realms of the human and the divine.

Another way to express this progressive shift in the soul's reality is to note how the soul experiences a kind of radical disintegration of its known personhood and a gradual ontological reintegration in God, which it will celebrate in the seventh dwelling places. This change is accomplished gradually by means of revelations and ecstasy, what we could call intellectual, emotional and physical experiences of the subjective reality of God that call into question any notions of reality that the soul might have up to this point. All of these experiences are ways in which a final purification of the soul's desire for union is effected in the soul. The intensity of the experiences combined with the hypersensitivity of the soul leave the soul in a state of serious vulnerability and fragility, in which it can paradoxically discover deep inner strength and a disintegration of boundaries. This process results in a complete reconfiguring of what constitutes the soul's selfhood; it is the full realization of relationality, where self and Other form a unitive process, as well as a unitive identity.

As the soul's desire for union with God is purified, its focus intensifies, burning throughout the soul as a kind of final crucible of loving desire. The searing yearning for fulfillment is profound and powerful; the soul suffers with impatience for total union with God, a desire that only intensifies with its brief encounters with God throughout these dwelling places:

> But the Spouse does not look at the soul's great desires that the betrothal take place, for He still wants it to desire this more, and He wants the betrothal to take place at a cost; it is the greatest of blessings. And although everything is small when it comes to paying for this exceptional benefit, I tell you, daughters, that for

the soul to endure such delay it needs to have that token or pledge of betrothal that it now has. O God help me, what interior and exterior trials the soul suffers before entering the seventh dwelling place! (VI:1:1)

The soul's acute restlessness is akin to the intense, perhaps even frantic search of the bride when she wanders about looking for the bridegroom in Song of Songs 3:1–3 and again in 5:5–8.[29] At this stage in the journey, passion has overcome reason, and the soul's heightened sensitivity, which has been increasing since the fourth dwelling places, moves into a form of self-abandonment, a radical loss of control over its circumstances and even its own identity, which is becoming bound up in the identity of God. Again, however, this process does not reflect only a surrendering of selfhood but also the soul's fullest embrace of a new understanding of self-in-God. The soul is also not passive in this process. Instead, it is actively engaged—through the cultivation, maintenance and expression of its desires—in its own transformation.

Edward Howells makes similar observations about this transformative process, which he rightly characterizes as the soul's gradual assimilation of the dynamism of the Trinity. He writes:

> The first [trinitarian] element, the dynamism of the Trinity, is found in Teresa's many references to the "force and "power" with which the soul is drawn to God in its depth in the various apprehensions of the sixth dwelling place. Through these apprehensions the soul acquires an increased deep "movement" belonging to the Trinity.[30]

The soul truly suffers a form of disintegration in the sixth dwelling places, because it is undergoing a final purification that threatens its identity as individual. Indeed, Teresa uses the word *deshacer* in this dwelling places; she speaks of the soul being "undone" or "dissolved," becoming unraveled like a ball of yarn, in order to be knitted into the fabric of Being itself, God. Desire itself fuels this disintegration, as she writes: "This action of love is so powerful that the soul dissolves with desire, and yet it doesn't know what to ask for since clearly it thinks that its God is with it" (VI:2:4). Consumed by its desire for consummation, the soul's temporary unitive experiences of God reinforce its own incompletion in and of itself. The yearning indicates the soul's painful lack of fulfillment at the same time that it suggests the possibility of fulfillment in its new identity as a self-with-God. Desire to bring that potential into being, becomes, at this stage, the labor and birthpangs of the soul's movement into the reality of God.

The soul suffers both internal and external trials in these dwelling places; the internal trials go to the very heart of its identity, while the external trials teach it to seek consolation only in God. When Teresa treats of the external trials the soul experiences (VI:1:3–5), she reveals how the soul has turned the critical corner of de-personalizing life's challenges and seeing all things that would have been a "crisis" before as a grace-filled opportunity to learn:

> This is an amazing truth. Blame does not intimidate the soul but strengthens it. Experience has already taught it the wonderful gain that comes through this path. It feels that those who persecute it do not offend God; rather that His Majesty permits persecution for the benefit of the soul. And since it clearly experiences the benefits of persecution, it acquires a special and very tender love for its persecutors. It seems to it that they are greater friends and more advantageous than those who speak well of it. (VI:1:5)

The soul struggles with the prestige she acquires as well as with the gossip, envy, and strife her reputation generates. This is an indication that the soul is moving past an individually sustained identity, as it shies away from external events that would highlight the soul's particularity.

There is no consolation here, unfortunately, for the soul only understands the necessity of this stage after the fact. And its usual remedies—vocal or mental prayer, solitude or company—do not compensate for the intense dissatisfaction it feels at its own ontological incompletion. Teresa writes that, at this stage, the soul "goes about with a discontented and ill-tempered mien that is externally very noticeable" (VI:1:13). The whole point of this stage and its trials is to increase the soul's desire and single-mindedness, for "before He belongs to it completely He makes it desire Him vehemently by certain delicate means the soul itself does not understand" (VI:2:1).

The soul is entering into the deep reality of the Song of Songs, having experienced not simply an erotic awakening but, now, a deepening knowledge of the erotic reality of God. It is wounded with a desirous love that seeks total consummation, even though, at the level of the sixth dwelling places, it is not yet able to bear such intensity for long. Indeed, Teresa likens the wound described above to a form of cauterization, noting: "it's as though from this fire enkindled in the brazier that is my God a spark leapt forth and so struck the soul that the flaming fire was felt by it" (VI:2:4). But the soul is not quite ready to be set on fire with love; it receives the spark but cannot enkindle it. Then, after the spark dies out, it is left in the disappointing space of wanting desperately to be set afire without any means of attaining its desire.[31] This experience is necessary, again, to increase the soul's resolution and determination to attain full union with God, to set aside any impediments to its totality. The soul's erotic desire is here purified, refined, and focused. In this process *eros* itself is gathering force within the soul to propel the soul into the fullness of erotic being.

Teresa spends chapter 3 describing locutions, or divine communication, along with the signs that reveal that they are authentic words from God. These locutions communicate the reality of God with a kind of concreteness that the soul has not experienced, and it is their very specificity that often aroused suspicion and skepticism. So Teresa describes several different indicators to provide readers with the means both to interpret them and to defend them, if necessary. Because locutions produce demonstrable effects on the soul, she argues, they are one of the ways that we know God mystically. In characterizing their effects on the soul, Teresa is concurrently describing part of the soul's own ontological transformation in the sixth dwelling places.

The first sign of authentic communication from God, described in VI:3:5, might be understood as experiential truth. The soul receives a message or revelation that brings with it some embodied communication of the subjective truth of the message. The statement resonates within the soul as ontologically true, not merely an abstraction. It is emotionally true as well as intellectually true. To understand this dimension of truth we cannot understand things as simply true or false (objectively) but rather as true because they have been incarnated and experienced and, in that process of becoming "real," they reveal something of their divine source. The soul understands their "truth," then, not simply because what is revealed can be conceptualized or has been demonstrated, but, more importantly, because the soul knows itself to have experienced God's self-communication. What God communicates to the soul incarnates itself within the heart, mind, and body of the recipient, causing some kind of transformation or growth in the human person. Thus, we could say that, in experiencing the truth of a locution, the person also experiences a co-creative moment in which God's words implant new life and deeper fullness of life in the human person. What Teresa does not say here, probably because she was unaware of more specialized speculative discussion of the Trinity, is that the intuitive understanding of human–divine communication she reveals in this section suggests that the soul is gradually learning the operations of the Trinity, not abstractly but through momentary participation in God's self-communication.[32]

The second sign (VI:3:6) of an authentic locution is that a deep form of peace is communicated to the soul through divine words that have a liberating effect on the soul, as in the scriptural text, "And you shall know the truth, and the truth shall set you free" (John 8:32). The transformative effect of God's self-communication liberates us from forms of internal and/or external oppression and thus establishes a deeper sense of safety and rest and peace, tranquility rather than internal forms of confusion or distress. We experientially now know that new life is possible and we acquire a deep peace in the knowledge that a mysterious process of transformation is occurring within us. The transformation is being brought about in us; we are an integral part of it yet it is beyond us and out of our control as well. All we can do is wonder and consent, open ourselves up to the mystery of it and recognize the awesome truth of it.

The third sign (VI:3:7) is the sense in which an experiential/essential/ontological truth is "imprinted in the memory" and therefore *eternal*. Thus this truth is an entryway into a *kairos* moment, a transcendent moment of ascent into the shared space of the mind of God and our mind, an experience in which God's thoughts or ideas are given to us and we participate briefly in that creative process that *is* the mind of God. Revelation of this sort is a critical, yet still momentary form of participation in what will be a deeper, ontological participation in the Trinity once we enter the seventh dwelling places. In other words, through locutions, the reality of God's being pierces our own being, creating openings through which we ourselves will be able, eventually, to enter into the reality of God's being. The glimpses that locutions give us into this ontological reality prepare us for the Trinitarian indwelling to be experienced in the center of the soul. Over time, these fragmentary revelatory experiences form a holistic realization of the being we share with God, at God's invitation. So, we find ourselves, at this stage, straddling existential and ontological reality, and the very substance of our life becomes increasingly punctuated by dartlike permeations of pure love, the very essence of God. In this process, we are being prepared for the entrance into our essential self and total union with the Trinity, which Augustine had affirmed resides vestigially in the soul.[33]

The signs of an authentic intellectual vision (VI:3:12–16) are similar, although, Teresa asserts, the intellectual vision is even more "supernatural" or profound than the locution. And the soul remains even more deeply convinced that it has experienced the presence of God because "our intellect could not compose them [the words imparted in the intellectual vision] so quickly" (VI:3:15) and "together with the words, in a way I wouldn't know how to explain, there is often given much more to understand than is ever dreamed of without words" (VI:3:16).

In chapter 4 Teresa discusses rapture as a way of being drawn out of one's senses—to protect it, as it were, from the intensity of being brought to union with God. It is a type of final purification, a more intense experience of burning from the spark, leaving a feeling of being stunned, bewildered, or overcome by the intensity of the experience.

> It seems that His Majesty from the interior of the soul makes the spark we mentioned increase, for He is moved with compassion in seeing the soul suffer so long a time from its own desire. All burnt up, the soul is renewed like the phoenix, and one can devoutly believe that its faults are pardoned. Now that it is so pure, the Lord joins it with Himself, without anyone understanding what is happening except these two. (VI:4:3)

The raptures are another way of communicating to the soul and imprinting in it the greatness of God, in the revelatory pieces—not the fullness—that we can assimilate at this stage, and which are necessary to prepare us for the fullness to come.

Teresa reminds us that raptures are disruptive by nature, disturbing and disquieting. They require great courage in the soul to stay with the intensity of the experience.

> Do you think it is a small disturbance for a person to be very much in her senses and see her soul carried off (and in the case of some, we have read, even the body with the soul) without knowing where that soul is going, what or who does this, or how? (VI:5:1)

The soul is completely thrown out of its ordinary routine and perspective on life and its meaning. Its radical disorientation/reorientation is necessary to establish complete ontological trust, not just in God but in God's way of being and the cosmos's cooperation with

God—even God's presence around and through people who consciously resist God's operation in the world.

Teresa describes this process of total trust, telling the soul who has "with such willingness offered everything to God" to "understand that in itself it no longer has any part to play." The soul here must be "determined now to do no more than…abandon itself into the hands of the one who is all powerful, for it sees that the safest thing to do is to make a virtue of necessity" (VI:5:2). Here, too, is where Teresa introduces the metaphor of the soul being a helpless ship, mercilessly tossed about in a tempest.

> Here this great God, who holds back the springs of water and doesn't allow the sea to go beyond its boundaries, lets loose the springs from which the water in this trough flows. With a powerful impulse, a huge wave rises up so forcefully that it lifts high this little bark that is our soul. A bark cannot prevent the furious waves from leaving it where they will; nor does the pilot have the power, nor do those who take part in controlling the ship. (VI:5:3)

This is an awesome experience in the deepest sense of the word, so "great courage is necessary" (VI:5:4).

For it is not only that the soul is being pulled out of itself and into the reality of God, where it experiences bliss, meaning, and full absorption. It is also that the soul is, in contrasting moments, reentering the depths of human reality—its own and all of human history—apparently alone and without the accompanying presence of God to give it the kind of strength it experiences in moments of union. In the moments of "reentry," the soul experiences the darkest wounds and shadows of human existential reality; as the bounds of selfhood disintegrate, the soul takes into itself human pain and suffering *writ large.* In accepting a greater, more universal human identity the soul relinquishes control of its existential identity much as Christ did on the cross. The flip side, of course, is that the soul gains an ontological identity with God, but the soul cannot yet completely see this. All it knows with certainty is that it is truly not in control of its own destiny, as much as it might like to be, and it is keenly aware of its own inadequacy, apart from God, to manifest God's presence in its personhood.

Teresa has suggested throughout the text that the soul and God will be united in the seventh dwelling places, and this is true. But the location of that union, like the union of humanity and divinity in Christ, will not merely be cosmic—within the "heaven" that Teresa calls the soul—but it will also be physical—within the embodied human person. In the sixth dwelling places, then, the soul is not simply growing in its consciousness of God's presence; it is also manifesting and becoming God's presence in its own personhood. Its own *incarnational potential* is being constructed in it, piece by piece, and it is gaining the strength to embody God. The soul must become fully aware not just of the experiences of God but of their *meaning,* and this can happen only when *intellectus* (the soul's ability to know) is fully reintegrated with *affectus* (the soul's ability to love), forming a new kind of loving wisdom within the soul. Visions and raptures are the vehicles for this integration; visions perhaps leaning more toward *intellectus* and raptures perhaps leaning more toward *affectus.* But there is no tension between the two; instead each is becoming bound to the other within the body and soul in its center. It is the intensity and integration of visionary experiences as a way of apprehending God that characterizes the sixth dwelling places, and this process may take a great deal of time. Indeed, in reflecting on her own experiences, Teresa recalls that she experienced the favors of the sixth dwelling places as early as forty years before, that is, in 1537, when she was just twenty-two.[34] But she could not understand their meaning or how they fit into the movement of her soul toward union with God, that is, how they were ontologically transformative and had been so in her life, until she had reached the stage of the sixth dwelling places. Teresa's desire to help readers who might similarly be struggling to understand the dynamics of this process accounts for her previous detail about the signs of true experiences of God, especially how they remain in the memory and thus can continue to convey their power and insight years later.

At another point Teresa suggests that visions here, which she describes as imaginary rather than intellectual (VI:5:7), are more than revelations of truth. They are also actual encounters with God, experiences of the Betrothed, and

> These meetings remain so engraved in the memory that I believe it's impossible to forget them until one enjoys them forever, unless they are forgotten through one's own most serious fault. But the Spouse who gives them has the power to give the grace not to lose them. (VI:5:11)

It is important to think of the visions Teresa describes as insights into God, gained from direct contact with God. They are multidimensional experiences that convey truth, meaning, understanding, even comprehension and apprehension of God in the soul's depths.

The ontological truth of these experiences then raises, for Teresa, the thorny issue of the soul's ontological security. She grants that the human person always has the possibility, as a human, to fall away from grace. But, by this moment in the soul's development, once past the cocoon and butterfly stages, a transformation has occurred such that moving out of the presence of God is highly unlikely. This presence—which, of course, has always been part of the soul's essential nature—has been increasingly recognized by the soul as it moves closer to the seventh dwelling places; now it is becoming fully realized ontologically in the soul, engendering a sense of deep, soul-safety in God. And this kind of radical trust is necessary for the intimate exchanges of the nuptial chamber of the seventh dwelling places. So the soul feels a radical confidence in God that emboldens it to speak freely, appreciatively and, indeed, glowingly about the magnanimous nature of God's love as spouse.

Further, this preparation for ontological union must be rooted in the fullness of the human person, body and soul. So, in the sixth dwelling places we see a gradual and progressive revelation of God's Godness not simply through visions, locutions, and raptures that draw the soul out of itself, but also through understandings and experiences of God's Godness in human form. Thus, by the sixth chapter of the sixth dwelling places, the glimpses of God we have gained through vision and rapture are forming a whole that is the incarnate reality of God, gradually being built into the human person experientially. For if the soul is truly united with God, it will come to incarnate God's presence in its being, and thus must enter into the fullest reality of God, a living Trinity. It has no way to do this without assimilating, through union with Christ, the fully human, fully divine identity of Christ. Visions and rapture, then, are this very "apprehension" of God's being.

Edward Howells sees in these strong movements of the spirit, the soul's momentary participation in the dynamism of the Trinity. Commenting on the impulses of love the soul feels for God, he observes:

> In another impulse, the "flight of the spirit," a swift movement is felt like a "huge wave," as the soul is swept up into God's infinitely greater power. Gradually, the soul becomes better accommodated to these favors and finds that it can appropriate this dynamism in order to love God in return....showing a pattern of activity which is clearly trinitarian, even though it is not yet explicitly recognized as such.[35]

In chapter 6 Teresa discusses how the way of rapture is perceived to be a "dangerous" path, but the soul "has found this path to be so greatly beneficial" that "even if it wanted to, it could not really desire anything else but to abandon itself into God's hands" (VI:6:2). Her defense of this path reflects her understanding that the full integration of our deepest passions and desires for connections—the most intense yearnings of our soul—with all other elements of our personhood is critical in making progress toward total union. From the union of wills to, now, the union of loving desire, the soul has been exploring the reality that our deepest passions and desires do not lead us away from God, but rather are given to us by God in order to bring us into God. But the consummation of its desires in God still remains beyond its grasp; the soul as butterfly "is unable to find a lasting place of rest; rather, since the soul goes about with such tender love, any occasion that enkindles this fire more makes the soul fly aloft" (VI:6:1). It is left unable to "desire anything else but to abandon itself into God's hands" (VI:6:2). Rapture, then, is the movement toward a "purification of desire" in which, through ongoing experiences of God's love, the soul is drawn into an experiential understanding of the concurrently agapic and erotic nature of God's love. The soul is united with God not only as an entity but also with the God who encompasses all movement; therefore, the knowledge of God the soul assimilates is concurrently an apprehension of God's way of loving. Subjectively felt within the soul through the union of tender love and intense desire, these experiences of rapture capacitate the soul even further, moving it toward deeper unitive experiences of God and toward the development of more united forms of agapic and erotic love within itself. The experiential knowledge of both of those subjective realities moves it more fully into the flowing love of God, an experience of reality in which there is no qualitative difference between *eros* and *agapē*.[36]

The joy of this form of love, new to the soul, is "so excessive the soul wouldn't want to enjoy it alone." Thus the soul both radiates this love outward and draws people to it as if in a communal celebration. "It seems it has found itself and that, like the father of the prodigal son, it would want to prepare a festival and invite all because it sees itself in an undoubtedly safe place, at least for the time being" (VI:6:10). Rapture, then, has the effect, ultimately, not of privatizing the soul's relationship with God, even though it deepens the intimacy that God and the soul share. Additionally, however, the soul is becoming the overflowing fountain Teresa used in the fourth dwelling places to typify divine activity, allowing the love of God to enter the world more fully. As the metaphor of the father of the prodigal son also suggests, the soul's mediating function in the world is bi-directional: in addition to serving as a medium for the outpouring of God, the soul also invites other humans toward the celebration of unitive possibility. The community that develops as a result of this soul's interactions in the world can be understood as a kind of affective circle, where loving affection is passed from one member to another in an agapic celebration; prayer, loving concern, empathic commitment, honesty, and integrity are the hallmarks of this community. Such communities allow us, as individuals, to appreciate and nurture the evolving human–divine relationship essential to humanity's ultimate well-being (see VI:6:11–12).

Teresa ends this section with a word of encouragement for such a community and a prayer for souls in this state: "Let us all help this soul, my daughters. Why do we want to have more discretion? What can give us greater happiness? And may all creatures help us forever and ever, amen, amen, amen!" (VI:6:13). The universal community described here requires forms of *abandonment*—of concern for external appearances, of criticism, of competition, of any sort of limitation to human potential—and offers radical *freedom,* in which no form of existential subjection can—or can be allowed to—deter humanity from its ultimate purpose, essential, incarnational union with God.

At the beginning of chapter 7 Teresa doubles back and asserts that the soul's joy at these experiences of freedom and deeper union only reinforce its understanding of the fragile state of humanity. For such a sensitive soul, sins are "always…alive in the memory, and this is a heavy cross" (VI:7:2). These memories carry with them the stab of compunction that triggers further gratitude and love for not ultimately being "lost," despite its own tendency to "wander" from grace. Although such memories of sin and the feelings they inspire are real, the soul at the same time feels deep gratitude for what it has learned about itself and life and God and can perhaps cultivate a kind of compassionate self-acceptance that is able to acknowledge that its mistakes were an essential part of that learning process. Since it knows that God ultimately does not impute blame for those mistakes, but rather looks more for signs of love behind and within the soul's actions and life choices, blanketing everything in love, it has learned to imitate that kind of compassion even toward self.[37]

In this chapter, too, Teresa is clear and forceful about her position that spiritual progress does not entail disembodiment. Meditation does not move from immanence to transcendence, and one does not reflect on the essence of God rather than the embodied life of Christ, whether in scripture or as it is being lived out in the present moment.

"To be always withdrawn from corporeal things and enkindled in love is the trait of angelic spirits, not of those who live in mortal bodies," she writes, rather tartly (VI:7:6). Teresa asserts here that searching for and seeing Christ in life experiences *is* seeing God, the encounter with Christ in the world and the self and the other is a living in the presence of God; indeed, she suggests that this is the only way she has found true and meaningful union (VI:7:6).

In considering and contemplating its own life narrative as a story of God's love, the soul recalls not only its own personal sin but also the experience of grace and the peace of forgiveness. The memory of God's love, contained in the intellect, inflames the will with desire; this is hardly a disembodied process, as the memory of love is mediated by incarnated experiences of love. So Teresa advises her readers continually to seek out God incarnationally, "as the Bride did in the Song of Songs" (VI:7:9). The soul need not wait for revelation or infused prayer but can always benefit here either from discursive meditation on moments in the life of Christ and their experience/meaning in contemporary life experiences (VI:7:10) or from moving through the memory into the meaning of personal encounters with Christ incarnate. Such an approach to prayer allows a person to walk "continually in an admirable way with Christ, our Lord, in whom the divine and the human are joined and who is always that person's companion" (VI:7:9).

Thus, although the favors of unitive encounters and all of their revelatory insights are critical to the transformation of the soul, the soul does not simply wait passively until such experiences come to it. It can also move itself into the divine presence through reflection on the humanity of Christ. This suggests that human–divine encounters are both exterior to and interior to the soul, and that both humanity and divinity serve as mediums for union. An important, if implicit, theological argument is forming here, that the incarnate God provides the vehicle to explore the fullness of humanity and the fullness of divinity as a single, integrated process. Probing the reality of the incarnation provides the bridge between the perspectival differences that have plagued the soul in its unitive encounters up to this point.[38] Christ is now being presented as a figure who mediates not only the human and the divine, within and outside the soul's sense of itself, but also as the bridge between mediated and immediate experience of union, as Edward Howells suggests:

> We see the intimate combination of divine and human, immediate and mediated, in this view of union: the favors received in the interior are already in the human-divine form of Christ, so that Christ *mediates* between divinity and our humanity, and yet we receive this union of nature immediately from God.[39]

It is in chapter 8 that Teresa describes the effects of such a habit of contemplation: the soul actually moves into the presence of the incarnate God. Teresa describes how, at this stage, the soul "will feel Jesus Christ, our Lord, beside it. Yet it doesn't see Him, neither with the eyes of the body nor with those of the soul. This is called an intellectual vision; I don't know why." Teresa reveals that when she first experienced this consciousness of presence she could not even understand it as a vision, "since she could not see anything" (VI:8:2). She also could not doubt the validity of the vision, partly because of its effects and partly because of its length. Here she distinguishes between intellectual and imaginary visions, explaining that this vision "lasted for many days, and once even for more than a year" (VI:8:3). This vision "imparts a special knowledge of God to the soul"; as Teresa analyzes these experiences of visions, she describes them as experiences of transformative companionship. She writes:

> This continual companionship gives rise to a most tender love for His Majesty, to some desires even greater than those mentioned to surrender oneself totally to His service, and to a great purity of conscience because the presence at its side makes the soul pay attention to everything. For even though we already know that God is present in all we do, our nature is such that we neglect to think of this. Here the truth cannot be forgotten, for the Lord awakens the soul to His presence beside it....[T]he

soul goes about almost continually with actual love for the One who it sees and understands is at its side. (VI:8:4)

The soul's gradual comprehension of Christ's ongoing companionate presence becomes, concurrently, a means for the soul to gain a new perspective on its own ontology, beginning to see, within itself, the union of human and divine embedded within it through the creative process and revealed to it incarnationally in Christ.[40] A kind of dwelling in divine presence is becoming more "normative" for the soul, based on its increasing companionship with Christ. And the mutuality of its relationship with Christ demonstrates its increasing capacitation for mutuality with God, emblematic of a life within the Trinity.[41]

If this vision is intellectual, according to the categories established by Augustine, it is no less real, tangible, and, most importantly, transformative for the soul morally, intellectually, and even incarnationally. Capitalizing on the idea that the soul, through the companionship of Christ, receives a "particular knowledge of God" (VI:8:4), Edward Howells suggests that Teresa here implies "that the soul is able to distinguish the persons in the Trinity," knowing God as Christ does. In other words, the soul "is now capable of knowing God in union *in the same act* as distinguishing itself from God, and this is a trinitarian activity."[42] The knowledge of God the soul now enjoys is possible only because it is moving into its incarnational potential, a potential it shares with Christ but into which it must be led through Christ.[43] As Howells notes,

> The soul's relation to the Father is that of the Son, in the bond of the Holy Spirit in the Trinity. This explains why the soul cannot now see God without also seeing itself: it is in a trinitarian relation to God in which the distinction between them cannot be seen without also seeing the unity of their relationship.[44]

Although the soul achieves a kind of perspectival breakthrough with this new form of companionate intellectual vision, *imaginative* visions do not cease. This is quite significant, because it signals Teresa's difference from her contemporaries, following Augustine, that intellectual visions were superior to imaginative ones. Their judgment was that imaginative visions allowed for greater human deception, or, as Teresa paraphrases manuals on the discernment of spirits, "they say the devil meddles more in these than in the ones mentioned, and it must be so." But because imaginative visions allow the soul, through the humanity of Christ, literally to step into its potential to incarnate God, Teresa cannot say that the "truly alive" presence of Christ they communicate to the soul is no longer necessary once the soul has seen God also through the eyes of Christ's divinity. Instead, she claims that they "seem to me more beneficial because they are in greater conformity with our nature" (VI:9:1). These imaginative visions are revelatory insights into the incarnate reality of God, from the mediated perspective of humanity. What this suggests is that the visionary experiences of the sixth dwelling places invite the soul into a form of movement from Christ's human perspective to Christ's divine perspective in intensifying contemplation that gradually blurs any boundary between the two perspectives and invites the soul into Christ's own unified way of being fully human and fully divine.

Movement into this integrated way of seeing reality gives the soul a changed self-perception and a more deeply integrated, incarnationally based perspective on humanity and divinity, revealed in and through Christ. This changing perspective can perhaps best be characterized as "reconciliatory"; it is grounded in an understanding that the ontological connection between humanity and divinity is stronger than any division between God and humanity caused by human sin. The perspectival breakthrough of the greater continuity of humanity and divinity provokes new insights into all theological questions. As a result, the soul comes to revise many of its previous perspectives on God and human nature, given its post-revelatory perspective on all reality. We can certainly see this revisionary process in Teresa's work. As Edward Howells notes, there is a "marked development" in Teresa's thought, one that he alternately characterizes as "a profound alteration" and a more developed theological understanding dependent on her "own progress and her experience of union." After a detailed analysis of the development of Teresa's thought, Howells concludes:

> She points to the dynamism of Christ's own union of natures and has access to the inner overflowing force of unity in the Trinity as the elements which are gradually developed in the soul in the process of transformation and found ultimately in the center of the soul.[45]

This gradual transformation within the soul, rooted in its mystical knowing of God and self, accounts for the new perspectives on human nature, Christ, and the Trinity.

The evolution in Teresa's theological thought is striking but not unique. As we suggested in the introduction, it bears a striking resemblance to the changing perspectives of Julian of Norwich, who found she had to rewrite completely sections of her *Showings* after twenty years of ongoing experiential insight into God led her to express the ontological reality of human-divine unity in more sophisticated ways. Specifically, Julian added a lengthy exploration of the Fall to the second version of the *Showings*, recasting it as a story of a lord and his servant whose relationship only deepens after the servant suffers a fall during his service to the lord. In examining the structure of the changes to Julian's thought reflected in the addition of the parable of the lord and the servant, Edmund Colledge and James Walsh conclude that unitive experiences of God, for Julian too, led to deeper reflection on human-divine activity and therefore an exploration of how the dynamics of the Trinity are taken into the soul's own identity. They write:

> The entire revelation develops Julian's mature thinking on what had become for her an obsessive problem, how what she knew to be true of sin, damnation and the anger of God can be reconciled with what she had been shown of the loving workings of mercy and grace upon the soul in contemplative union with God.[46]

As they explain, Julian's contemplative experience and the parable of the lord and the servant that epitomize her experience of the divine–human relationship serve, then, as the framework for an entire systematic theology, including Julian's explanation of how the relationship between God and human beings persists despite human inadequacy and frailty; how this contemplative relationship is trinitarian; how creation and redemption come together in Christ, the head of human nature; and how knowledge of God in Christ enables creatures to grow in understanding of their own nature, and to receive the gifts which flow from mutual indwelling.

For both women, unitive experiences of God and the contemplative life that grounds them stimulate theological creativity and a greater ability to express the dynamic, living reality of God working within humanity. The more integrated theological vision, particularly its trinitarian aspects, comes to the soul gradually, as it attunes itself to the presence of Christ communicated to it through visions. Describing this process, Teresa declares that through the experience of imaginative visions, the inner eye sees the presence of Christ, an experience of brilliance that inspires deep awe in the soul:

> Although the Lord's presence is the most beautiful and delightful a person could imagine even were he to live and labor a thousand years thinking about it (for it far surpasses the limitations of our imagination or intellect), this presence bears such extraordinary majesty that it causes the soul extreme fright. (VI:9:5)

After the stirring caused in the soul by this vision, there is a deep calm and peace left by the presence, and "this soul is left so well instructed about so many great truths that it has no need of any other master" (VI:9:10). Such peace serves as an important counterbalance to the inflamed desires of the soul to love God ever more fully at this stage. Further, repeated experiences of Christ's presence stimulate the soul's *constant recollection* of the incarnate God, which, in turn, reinforces the soul's knowledge of its essential nature in God.

Another form of vision, experienced in a suspended state, is one in which the soul sees experientially "how all things are seen in God and how God has them all in Godself" (VI:10:2). This theological reality remains imprinted in the soul and is recognized as an expression of ultimate Truth; indeed, it is accompanied by the knowledge that "God alone is Truth, unable to lie" (VI:10:5). The Truth that is God is everlasting, yet the soul is being invited to walk with that Truth as its companion. With such experiences, humility is again reinforced in the soul, now because "God is supreme truth; and to be humble is to walk in truth" (VI:10:7).

These many insights into ultimate reality leave the soul thoroughly "pierced" by a knowledge of God, experienced ecstatically. In chapter 11 Teresa returns to the butterfly/dove image recalling its dilemma: how much it wishes to use its wings to soar toward God and how, "even though it may have been receiving these favors for many years," it still "sees itself so distant and far from enjoying God." What it has learned through these insights is "how much this great God and Lord deserves to be loved," and this, in turn, increases the soul's desire to love. In this escalation of desire the soul has a sudden experience of ecstasy in its most intimate depths in which "this sudden flash of lightning reduces to dust everything it finds in this earthly nature of ours; for while this experience lasts nothing can be remembered about our being" (VI:10:2). Such experiences carry the soul out of itself (as self alone, not self-in-God) and, upon its return to itself as self, "It feels a strange solitude because no creature in all the earth provides it company, nor do I believe would any heavenly creature, not being the One whom it loves; rather, everything torments it" (VI:10:5). For Teresa the soul now "dies with the desire to die," since it believes that the human person is unable to contain the kind of union it so desires (VI:11:9).

The pain and even agony so eloquently described in the sixth dwelling places is perhaps best encapsulated by the reality of human fragmentation and incompletion. The soul has had enough experiences of God, at this point, to understand and feel deeply the tension between humanity's desire for unitive wholeness and its experience of partiality and fragmentation, reinforced by dualisms that permeate its ordinary experience of self and world. In unitive moments, such partiality is known to be illusory; in nonunitive moments, the soul struggles to maintain its unitive perspective. The movement back and forth between the wholeness it experiences in God and its own partiality as self, coupled with the naked vulnerability it has cultivated in its own essence, is experienced as pain, the pain inherent in the shattering of a selfhood predicated on individuality. Yet the experience and knowledge of completion and fulfillment bring a wholesome joy that counterbalances the pain. Gradually, over the course of many such movements, the tension between the two extremes is resolved as the soul is able to take into itself the fullness of self-in-God. Thus the soul is being changed ontologically through its growing knowledge of human potential and its experiential knowledge of the ultimate reality of the communion of all things in God. Its growing awareness of all that is occurring within it brings about a sense of greater relativity and patience. It is acquiring a trinitarian way of being, in which its own unity and dynamism replicate the unity and dynamism of God. Perhaps we could even say that the soul is participating actively in the birthing process of becoming in God, moving with the dynamic forces of divine loving power.

The
Seventh
Dwelling
Places

*I*F, IN THE SIXTH DWELLING PLACES, the soul has been brought out of itself repeatedly, drawn both into the presence of God's majesty and into the companionate presence of Christ, swelling its desire for some kind of explosive, unitive resolution, what it experiences in the seventh dwelling places is a stunningly quiet passage into the intimate being of the trinitarian God. The seventh dwelling places, as Teresa notes, are really God's dwelling place, "For just as in heaven so in the soul His Majesty must have a room where He dwells alone. Let us call it another heaven" (VII:1:3). Like the cellar in the Song of Songs, the soul must then be brought into its innermost chamber (VII:1:3), even though God's dwelling place is within its own deepest center. The union between God and the soul is, in the seventh dwelling places, a nonecstatic, permanent experience of God's indwelling presence. For, in the seventh dwelling places, all raptures cease; they have accomplished ontologically what they were intended to accomplish. The truth now flows wordlessly into the soul; revelatory knowledge of God, self, and world has become an ongoing way of seeing and knowing. Union, too, is no longer fleeting; the soul now lives in the ongoing presence of God, experienced both as a form of resting with the divine and moving with the divine. Here, instead of experiencing God partially, the soul is brought fully and completely into the trinitarian nature of God.

In this seventh dwelling place the union comes about in a different way: Our good God now desires to remove the scales from the soul's eyes and let it see and understand, although in a strange way, something of the favor he grants it. When the soul is brought into that dwelling place, the Most Blessed Trinity, all three Persons, through an intellectual vision, is revealed to it through a certain representation of the truth. (VII:1:6)

The soul is prepared for this revelation of God's nature first through "an enkindling in the spirit" and then, after a vision of each person of the Trinity in its separateness, "through an admirable knowledge the soul understands as a most profound truth that all three Persons are one substance and one power and one knowledge and one God alone." The knowledge of the trinitarian God is not abstract, even though "it knows in such a way that what we hold by faith, it understands, we can say, through sight," for at this point:

> All three Persons communicate themselves to it, speak to it, and explain those words of the Lord in the Gospel: that He and the Father and the Holy Spirit will come to dwell with the soul that loves Him and keeps His commandments. (VII:1:6)

It may strike some as curious that, although Teresa has not mentioned the Trinity at any previous point in the treatise, she clearly teaches that the culmination of the mystical journey is an entry into the reality of the Triune God. Some previous scholars have rightly noted this as one of the unique features of her mystical doctrine, and, if we are to appreciate fully Teresa's contribution to the Christian theological tradition, it is important to understand the significance of this orientation. As we have been noting throughout our theological review, Teresa's experiences of God thus far have focused on God and Christ without much reference to the Holy Spirit, who appears briefly in the sixth dwelling places as she discusses forms of divine communication (VI:3:16).[1] The bulk of her attention has been devoted to emphasis on the incarnate reality of God, in which she seems to privilege union with Christ. Indeed, if one were to read only the *Life* or the first six dwelling places of the *Interior Castle*, one would rightly characterize Teresa's mysticism as Christocentric and would anticipate that the descriptions of mystical union contained in the seventh dwelling places would involve nuptial language about Christ. However, the soul finds itself, instead, in the company of all three persons of the Trinity, in effect brought into the depths of the dynamism of God. Equally noteworthy, the soul experiences this company in an ongoing, sustained way, suggesting that the fullness of mystical union pulls the soul into God's eternal activity as well as God's eternal essence. Union with a God who is "both a noun and a verb" or the "self-communicating One" provides simple analogies for the trinitarian model of mystical union Teresa describes.

Thus, the material in the seventh dwelling places widens, deepens, and intensifies Teresa's previous insights into the divine nature and the extent to which humans can participate in it at an ontological level, sustaining as well as resting in divine activity, as in the states of being symbolized by Mary and Martha.[2] So here the soul moves with God even as it stays permanently in God's presence. Even more than representing contemplation, Mary may be seen as a symbol of God's permanent *indwelling* in creation, while Martha connotes God's creative, redemptive and renewing *activity* in the world. With this metaphor Teresa seems intent on conveying her own entry into the dynamic activity of God, even as she insists on the permanence of God's presence in the soul. The careful and protracted reflection on the nature of ecstasy in the sixth dwelling places makes a great deal more sense when examined in light of Teresa's particular characterization of mystical union. In the sixth dwelling places, she has described multiple states of being, into many (if not all) of which the soul must be introduced in order to sustain divine dynamism.

Once it has experiential knowledge of the Trinity and its full ontological reality has been revealed to the soul, Teresa writes that "the soul finds itself in this company every time it takes notice" (VII:1:9). Thus, a critical turning point has been made in the soul's capacity to see and know. Rather than experiencing God through partial revelations, the soul experiences God ontologically and, to its astonishment, what it previously experienced as moments of revelation has become its more normative, ongoing way of seeing and apprehending. It is introduced to the reality of God in such a way that it participates in this very reality of God. Teresa writes:

Each day this soul becomes more amazed, for these Persons never seem to leave it any more, but it clearly beholds, in the way that was mentioned, that they are within it. In the extreme interior, in some place very deep within itself, the nature of which it doesn't know how to explain, because of a lack of learning, it perceives this divine company. (VII:1:7)

And because this is not a momentary realization but a participation in an ontological reality, the soul is not drawn out of itself by this realization, nor is it completely overcome by and absorbed in this reality; rather, "the soul is much more occupied than before with everything pertaining to the service of God, and once its duties are over it remains with that enjoyable company" (VII:1:8). The soul now sees God face to face, able to behold God permanently; the seventh dwelling places is the realization of the "then" of Paul's famous passage on sight: "For now we see in a mirror dimly, but then face to face. Now I know in part; then I shall understand fully, even as I have been fully understood" (see 1 Cor 13:12).

The peace the soul experiences in this resolution of its previous ontological incompletion convinces it of the absolute truth of the experience, of the subjective reality it has come to know through its journey within, which is the ontological reality of God. And it rests with confident trust in that reality as absolute truth.[3] Teresa uses several Pauline texts to contextualize the union with God that has been achieved. First she describes union with God as "becoming one spirit with God" (see 1 Cor 6:17).[4] Then, returning to the metaphor of the butterfly, she describes how, after the waves of rapture that propelled it through the sixth dwelling places, it has now found repose in Christ and therefore has died to itself and lives in Christ.[5] The reader discovers that the butterfly has disappeared wordlessly, absorbed or taken into the reality of God, and Teresa gives us little insight into how this has happened, except to suggest that the barrier between it and God has been slowly disintegrating through the raptures of the sixth dwelling places. So now the soul is "almost always in quiet" without dryness or interior disturbances (VII:3:10), and it rarely, if ever, experiences rapture.[6]

The introduction into the soul's participation in the trinitarian reality is followed by the experience of spiritual marriage, in which God takes up residence in the interior depths of the soul, making the indwelling incarnate in the human person. This is a delicate experience—Teresa uses words like "sublime favor," "such extreme delight," and concludes, "I can say only that the Lord wishes to reveal for that moment, in a more sublime manner than through any spiritual vision or taste, the glory of heaven" (VII:2:3). The soul is made one with God in such a way that "just as those who are married cannot be separated, He doesn't want to be separated from the soul" (VII:2:3).

Unlike the union experienced in the state of spiritual betrothal (i.e., in the sixth dwelling places), where the two can be separated and remain by themselves, and where the union is bound by moments of time, here in the seventh dwelling places "the soul always remains with its God in that center" (VII:2:4). To reinforce this reality, Teresa uses metaphors of inseparability:

> In the spiritual marriage the union is like what we have when rain falls from the sky into a river or fount; all is water, for the rain that fell from heaven cannot be divided or separated from the water of the river. Or it is like what we have when a little stream enters the sea; there is no means of separating the two. (VII:2:4)

This union gives the soul aspirations in love that it knows are far beyond what it itself can generate, and through these aspirations "the soul understands clearly that it is God who gives life to our soul. These aspirations come very, very often in such a living way that they can in no way be doubted."[7]

The reality of this union sustains the soul in a life-giving, nurturing way that Teresa describes as continual nursing: "For from those divine breasts where it seems God is always sustaining the soul there flow streams of milk bringing comfort to all the people of the castle" (VII:2:6). The effect is a kind of "bathing" in the loving presence of God. Such metaphors of flow are suggestive of the relationship of persons within the Trinity, a metaphysical flow within which the soul lives and which it can now manifest in the world, despite the fragmentation and lack of flow within created matter. On a subjective level, the soul's engagement in trinitarian flow is felt most clearly in a permanent loving peace the soul feels within its own depths, as Teresa writes: "The soul, as I have said, does not move from that center nor is its peace lost; for the very One who gave peace to the apostles when they were together can give it to the soul" (VII:2:6).

If the soul has found its repose in the creative, redemptive, restorative life of the Trinity, who dwells in it, its life, too, is changed. The first effect of this new life, Teresa writes, "is a forgetfulness of self, for truly the soul, seemingly, no longer is, as was said" (VII:3:2). Perhaps the reality that the soul has found true rest then enables it to prioritize not its own rest but its love for others.

> For if it is with God very much, as is right, it should think little
> of itself. All its concern is taken up with how to please God more
> and how or where it will show God the love it bears God. This
> is the reason for prayer, my daughters, the birth always of good
> works, good works. (VII:4:6)

Impulses of love continue to flow through the soul, but they now flow out of its nature in God, and thus are not experienced as urgent, the way they are in the sixth dwelling places. Instead, they are manifestations of a flow of participatory grace in which the soul dwells, so they are gentle, expressions of the delicate but penetrating touch of God the soul enjoys constantly (see VII:4:8–9). The soul moves about now in a flow of erotic agape.

The soul's participation in the flow of loving energy that characterizes the Trinity is reflected in its balance between contemplation and action. Here, Teresa argues that "Martha and Mary must join together in order to show hospitality to the Lord and have Him always present....How would Mary, always seated at His feet, provide Him with food if her sister did not help her? His food is that in every way possible we draw souls" closer to God (VII:4:12). The relative ease with which the soul sustains both activity and unitive resting mirror the characteristics of God as both indwelling and yet constantly engaged in creating, sustaining, and renewing. This suggests that the metaphor of Mary and Martha might also be reflective of God's own ways of being, as expressed in and through the Trinity, at once unitive and self-diffusive. In learning these ways of being, the soul participates in the creative and redemptive activity of the Trinity, making this manifest incarnationally on earth. Lest this seem like a tremendously daunting task to her readers, Teresa reassures them that souls in the seventh dwelling places can do this easily, because "[t]his fire of love in you enkindles their souls, and with every other virtue you will be always awakening them" (VII:4:14).

Teresa is careful not to describe in much detail the experience of the soul in these dwelling places, for the soul has moved into a more wordless and direct communication with God. This is the wine cellar of consummation in the Song of Songs, where wine is both stored and yet flows freely, characteristic of the abundance of loving energy that flows in and through the soul as outpourings of its continual, intimate communication with God. "So in this temple of God, in this His dwelling place, He alone and the soul rejoice together in the deepest silence" (VII:4:11). In that rejoicing they look around at a world in sore need of manifestations of God's presence and begin to work together with a sense of deepest satisfaction and joy in all they are accomplishing together as partners. As Teresa concludes:

> In sum, my Sisters, what I conclude with is that we shouldn't build castles in the air. The Lord doesn't look so much at the greatness of our works as at the love with which they are done. And if we do what we can, His Majesty will enable us each day to do more and more. (VII:4:15)

Teresa ends by encouraging readers to "delight in this interior castle" often, for its door is always open and there are untold riches to be discovered within its depths. Indeed, she promises: "Once you get used to enjoying this castle, you will find rest in all things, even those involving much labor, for you will have the hope of returning to the castle, which no one can take from you" (Epilogue:2). Contemplation of the self empowers the soul to see more of the beauty of the God who created us with the capacity for the same kind of loving intimacy that actually brings goodness into being.

> Although no more than seven dwelling places were discussed, in each of these there are many others, below and above and to the sides, with lovely gardens and fountains and labyrinths, such delightful things that you would want to be dissolved in praises of the great God who created the soul in His own image and likeness. (cf. Epilogue:3)

Cultivation of loving relationship with the creator God mirrored within its depths thus empowers us, as individuals and as community, to construct lives of meaning and purpose, incarnating the presence of God in the world at large.

Walking with Teresa Today

*W*E HAVE ENTERED THE DEPTHS of the *Interior Castle,* discovering its culmination in the sacred center of the soul where the soul shares in the trinitarian life of intimate communication, not just with God but also with others. I have tried to move slowly through the progressive stages in the journey, highlighting in each of the seven dwelling places what is learned about self, God, relationality, and love. I have also tried to capture, through description and analysis, the increasingly complex tapestry of Teresa's prose. Beginning in the fourth dwelling places, as the soul's capacity to know expands, the strands of psychological, spiritual, and theological reflection thicken, becoming so intertwined by the fifth dwelling places that the words necessary to convey the many levels of experience form a carpet of language that obscures as much as it clarifies. Thus, in the short term, even though I have only touched the surface of what Teresa seeks to communicate of the relational reality of God known through the Trinity, I fear that I have lost those readers who picked up this book simply because they were curious about Teresa or sought spiritual edification. In my concluding remarks, then, I hope to re-connect more directly and forthrightly with those of you who favor the "less is more" approach.

The gradual introduction of theological ideas and terminology, which I have attempted to keep at a minimum, reflects the major underlying premise of Teresa's *Interior Castle,* which I want to state simply without undermining its profundity: the self is, in the deepest sense, a *theological construct* as much as a *social construct.* The latter point is clear to us. Contemporary biology, neurochemistry, genetics, and many other scientific disciplines may not be able to explain all of the complex processes that go into the formation and evolution of the human person, but they certainly make it impossible for us to conceive of the individual person as a *tabula rasa*. For well over a hundred years now psychologists have been making abundantly clear to us how much influence others have on our understanding of selfhood and how determinative their influence can be in our ability to grow and flourish as human persons. But it is less clear to us that the process of discovering, defining, and becoming a self is also inherently a process of discovering and naming possibility and divine presence or absence in the human person and in human history.

Using the most basic theological language—that the soul is God's dwelling place—provides Teresa with a starting point to show how the process of fashioning an individual life—the task of living—is inherently theological. It is a construction of human reality, an exploratory living out of possible realities in, through, and beyond historical causality, a process I refer to using the Christian tradition's language of "incarnating." I use this verb actively to convey the ongoing process of incarnation. For, as Teresa makes clear, if the soul is God's dwelling place, then the soul is the space in which God becomes more real, just as the human person grows into his or her deepest reality. This process is God's ongoing "becoming" in the world.

Incarnating is germane to humanity, as humanity: we embody matter, thoughts, ideas, and principles, and make them concretely real through our human activity as embodied persons. Indeed, the fact that we do this whether or not we realize it—the reality that much of our human activity is not fully intentional but rather reactive or disconnected from our fullest consciousness—is the cause of Teresa's initial lament in the first dwelling places. Recall her plea to greater self-knowledge and intentionality:

> It is a shame and unfortunate that through our own fault we don't understand ourselves or know who we are. Wouldn't it show great ignorance, my daughters, if someone when asked

who he was didn't know, and didn't know his father or mother or from what country he came? Well now, if this would be so extremely stupid, we are incomparably more so when we do not strive to know who we are, but limit ourselves to considering only roughly these bodies. Because we have heard and because faith tells us so, we know we have souls. But we seldom consider the precious things that can be found in this soul, or who dwells within it, or its high value. (I:1:2)

What Teresa is lamenting here is not so much human ignorance of Christian doctrine (i.e., what "faith tells us") nor even our embodied state, but the fact that we let anything other than our deepest human capacities—capacities "we seldom consider," much less consciously develop—determine our behavior in the world. This is most fundamentally, then, a call to human consideration of the possibility of its divine origins and the capacity of each human person to mediate in some way divine presence through his or her life.

Without denying that Teresa played a significant (and intentional) role in the Catholic Counter-Reformation and that a Catholic interpretive system guided her understanding of human life, the fact that she identified the interior depths of the human person as the primary sphere of human-divine intimate creativity suggests that her insights contribute to a deeper sense of what it is to be human, not merely what it means to be Christian or Catholic. Thus, although Teresa clearly felt that Christian theology offered the best framework for her to understand and express the human–divine relationship, it is not clear that her theological system, as explicitly Christian as it is, is unable to enter a larger interreligious dialogue about the nature of the self, especially the self and the self-beyond-self as points of entry into human–divine relationality or ultimate reality.

This leads to the corollary to Teresa's major premise, that understanding the self is a theological project requiring some forms of theological language. As Bernard McGinn has cogently argued, the mystical life cannot be separated from a religious tradition that provides a symbol system, a sacred text, and an interpretive framework to facilitate the human person's understanding of experiences of ultimacy. Religious traditions do not contain all the answers to the questions that human life provokes, but their theological systems do provide language that enables us to pose the questions we must ask to explore the possible meanings of experiences. Within contemplative practice, as the borders of selfhood expand, we need a language that allows for exploration both of self-transcending experiences and for consideration of the expansion of immanence. Mystics have always struggled to express the ineffable, and their linguistic experiments have often generated controversy within religious systems. What mystical traditions demonstrate so clearly, however, is the evolving process of human understanding of the divine, even of divine–human interaction, requiring sensitivity and openness to the ongoing transformation of religious understanding and the human capacity to know, at the levels both of the human person and of the religious community.

If the human person has the capacity to see, know, and express God, bringing those insights back out into the world of human activity is the flip side of "incarnating" as active verb. In words and deeds, revelatory knowing is moved through the human person, so that humans themselves, as well as God, participate in revealing the divine to others. As we noted, Teresa ends the *Interior Castle* with something of an admonition:

> In sum, my Sisters, what I conclude with is that we shouldn't build castles in the air. The Lord doesn't look so much at the greatness of our works as at the love with which they are done. And if we do what we can, His Majesty will enable us each day to do more and more, provided that we do not quickly tire. (VII:4:15)

For Teresa, theological insights matter only when their implications are applied to human behavior. The inner peace of the seventh dwelling places is not an ethereal tranquility, rooted in avoidance or escapism. Teresa's political and ecclesiastical circumstances were at least as troubled as our own, and Teresa understood it to be both her duty and her desire to be engaged actively in working for the greater good of church and society. Thus, for her, revelations, ecstasy, and all of the forms of divine communication in the sixth dwelling places are not simply experiences to be savored but rather transformative activity within the soul that the soul then moves into the world. An ecstatic life, as Teresa helps us to understand it, is participation in human-divine transformative activity in the world, and it is as much a privilege and a joy as a form of suffering and work. Indications of the celebratory nature of incarnating include Teresa's identification of the soul with the father of the prodigal son, who rejoices in redemptive work. Recalling the joy inherent in the process of transformation toward the good is critical if we are to accompany one another and bring about the greater good within the human community. Teresa's insights, I suggest, allow us to move beyond stereotypical Christian expressions of self-abnegation and resignedly "taking up the cross" in order to engage in deeper explorations of the pleasures of enabling human flourishing.

The *Interior Castle* is a profound gift, offered to us by a woman of deep insight, wit, compassion, and heart. As we noted in the introduction, the *Interior Castle* is a book that easily might not have not been written. Teresa's dedication to understanding and expressing the vision of God she believed to have been gradually revealed to her through a lifetime of prayer was challenged not only by the inherent difficulties of the theological enterprise, but by the contemporary strictures on those who engaged in this enterprise: the narrowing of speculative theological discourse to those who were university educated and who wrote in Latin, the intense scrutiny of theological treatises, and the prejudices of her contemporaries against women as theological teachers and as competent practioners and interpreters of mental prayer. The specific circumstances of the *Interior Castle,* written shortly after the confiscation and review of her *Life* by the Inquisition in 1575, and her inquisitorial investigation in Seville in 1575–76 make all the more remarkable Teresa's even more extensive interior examination and theological apologia contained in the book. Indeed, Teresa's dedication to self-expression and theological exploration reinforce for us that the mystical journey is, by definition, a potentially subversive social activity, capable of transforming social and intellectual paradigms. Certainly, the mystical journey entails a deep commitment to truth and authenticity, a dedication to embodying, in time and space, the principles, values, and truths we experience in the depths of the inner self.

As Segundo Galilea observes: "The mystics remind us that the experience of God in history—which we are sincerely searching for today—is something essential to Christian identity. It is an arduous process, with its own special demands. Above all, it is an original and irreducible experience."[1] For Teresa, the experience of God led to a rejection of social norms and practices she understood to be unjust (for example, the exclusion of *conversos* from religious orders; the Carmelites avoided such a practice until after Teresa's death) as well as a restrained but lucid critique of institutions like the Inquisition that often hindered rather than helped Christians in their pursuit of authentic religiosity. Further, Teresa's larger visions of reform arose naturally from her commitment to the reform of self, guided by prayerful exploration of the meaning and purpose of her own human life. Indeed, in the nakedness of her self-expression, Teresa models a process for us, perhaps enabling us to negotiate our own movement, through the self, to explore the links between God and the history of humanity. As Galilea puts it:

> Whenever I read a passage from St. Teresa of Avila, I am convinced that God and the experience of God are as real as any object I can touch, or as any historical event I have witnessed. To read St. Teresa is to perceive that God truly exists as a reality that is present and can be experienced in our life, and not just as a rather convincing idea.[2]

As feminist thought has been emphasizing for decades, the construction of the self has significant political implications; what follows is that there is a direct correlation between the depth of self-transformation and the depth of social transformation. If, as Janet Ruffing suggests, "Mysticism is a transformative process that supports self-transcendence, the overcoming of too small a sense of self," it is also a catalyst to question any social factors that would encourage narrow definitions of the self, as she indicates: "The self discovered in mystical consciousness is a self related to Ultimacy, a self that is more than the self can imagine itself to be and surely more than any society conventionally wants it to be."[3]

The *Interior Castle*'s invitation to the discovery of a more authentic self is what has intrigued scholars of psychology for several decades now; they have been quick to appreciate Teresa for her capacity to express internal experiences with a clarity and profundity that convey deep appreciation for the complexities of the human psyche. Whether we examine Teresa's use of metaphors or her description of subjective states, as readers we can approach the book's spiritual and pastoral applications quite readily, comparing Teresa's schema of the human psyche with our own developing sense of self and locating ourselves in various places within the text. Further, Teresa's sensitivity to the dynamics of the internal world facilitates fruitful conversations between psychological and spiritual theory, particularly as they involve models of human development.

We should also be clear, however, that Teresa's sense of "self" was most likely rather different from the typical twenty-first-century Western one. Like Augustine, Teresa uses the "self" to speak about human nature more generally and even more universally. Although she recognizes that individuals have different paths toward God, she is clearly attempting to speak about the human–divine relationship through careful attention to her own experience as a self. Further, rather than seeing the self as ruggedly individualistic and completely autonomous, Teresa saw the self within the context of a community openly seeking the movement of God in its midst.

How are we to appropriate what Teresa has to teach us about self and God today? Teresa's initial insights into the tensions between a self constructed primarily on external values and superficial knowledge of one's internal capacities are significant in and of themselves. They suggest parallels with discussions of true and false self, the importance of intuition in evaluative decisions, and the diverse ways of knowing that must inform our growth as whole persons.[4] But an even greater contribution lies in her insistence that emotion and affective capacity be incorporated into the very definitions of cognition and consciousness. This argument, located in the fourth dwelling places, is the point of entry into exploration of the authentic self, and it can be placed into fruitful dialogue with the more holistic definitions of emotion and subjectivity emerging in recent scholarship.[5] The movement of the will into the expansion of the heart (or affective capacity) signals a commitment to authentic subjectivity, a willingness to allow emotions to guide us beyond the immediate level of feeling and into a realm of deeper awareness of the self and its relation to others. Entering empirically into this relational reality not only constitutes the deepest expression of being human; it is also the ultimate capacitation of humanity. Within this ontological space, we get a clearer sense of the self's own malleability, and the capacity for the transformation of self and society is ignited. At the same time, the complexity of interpreting emotion entails a greater need for partnership and accompaniment, both to counter the lack of perspective that one might have and to explore a fuller range of options in affective expression in all human relations.

Teresa teaches a model of prayer that reinforces the habit of introspection, even as it leads the individual far beyond self-absorption into a deeper understanding of the depths and capacities of humanity at large, from both an immanent and a transcendent perspective. The practice of Teresa's way of prayer is a continually deepening engagement in the "becoming" of creation. As Francis Gross notes, prayerful awareness of the kind Teresa teaches is

> primarily an awareness of God, the God within. It is a kind of resting in a divine embrace within one's self. It is a resting in love. It is also a surrender to God….This is the willingness which Gerald May opposes to its counter quality of willfulness. It is a willingness to follow the inner voice and to rest content in the presence of the author of that voice. If I infer correctly, that

inner voice is the joining of one's own voice with the divine voice.[6]

When one studies Teresa carefully, it is difficult not to conclude, with Gross, that psychology leads not only to spiritual questions but to the theological ones as well.

Perhaps because, within Christianity, we have long confused theology with product and doctrine or have been so involved in apologetic orientations of many sorts, there has been a certain hesitancy (Augustine aside) to incorporate into the canon of theological authorities those who are openly subjective and self-referential. Arguably, however, precisely because the *Interior Castle* takes the intricacy of subjective human experience so seriously, it also provides us with a systematic theological framework, one that takes as its point of departure that knowledge of the self leads to knowledge of God. If we explore this thesis in our own practical ways, we can begin to experience and know the truth of Teresa's deeper theological insights. Traditionally, those insights would be understood to fall within separate categories: what a theologian teaches about human nature (theological anthropology), about the nature of God (theology), and about Christ (christology). But the beauty of this text lies partly in the way these separate teachings have become interrelated dimensionalities of a larger whole: humanity, created in the image of God, is intimately related to God, not simply through a creative process in the past but through the ongoing recovery and exploration of the potentiality of that creative process—a redemption and transformation made possible as the human person forges a deeply loving and companionate relationship with the incarnate God. For Teresa, deep reflection and exploration of human nature will, over the course of a lifetime, literally turn a soul inside out, over and over again, pulling it into the depths of God deeply present in its own created nature while also pulling it into the divine activity of the Trinity. Similarly, reflection on the nature of God or the love of Christ invites the soul into a series of unitive encounters that facilitate the same experiential knowledge of human potentiality that is the mystery of incarnation.

Certainly, one of Teresa's greatest theological contributions is, then, her thorough and dynamic recovery of the fullness of the Christian doctrine of incarnation. In the *Interior Castle*, we have the means to explore the reality of human–divine union as both a mystery to be contemplated and, increasingly, a part of our day-to-day lives. The union of humanity and divinity, fully realized in Christ, becomes real and manifested in us as, gradually, we become accustomed to the presence of God we experience in contemplative prayer and action. Repeated experiences of that companionate presence convince the soul that God, through God's loving activity, is somehow bound up in human reality and can be known intimately in and through the multitude of experiences of self-other/Other relationality that human life makes possible.

In the *Interior Castle* Teresa teaches us to enter into our hearts, as the seat of God in humanity; to seek the wisdom that is contained there; and to cultivate, purify, and refine the desires of our hearts, allowing them to inform how we understand reality. On a concrete level, to do so is to allow the mystery of God that we intuitively recognize to seep slowly through the challenges, difficulties, and struggles of our life circumstances. In theological terms, we begin to see and live our lives as a beautiful series of encounters and opportunities to incarnate God's presence in the many intersections of relational spheres that surround us.

Teresa also encourages us to understand human life as the process of coming to know our souls as mysterious and powerful vessels of passion and peace, intertwined within the body of Christ into a greater fabric of being. Introduction into the depths of our personhood reveals both our interconnection with others and our absolute (but initially little-recognized) relationship with God. Teresa realized this, cognitively and practically, through a three-step process: she began by imitating what she understood to be God's way of being; she was transformed by her engagement in that way of being; and gradually she incarnated that very way of being.

Teresa lived out this theology, despite difficult sociopolitical circumstances, and thus made her life and her writing both contemplative and prophetic acts, knitted together seamlessly. This, too, is part of her theological and pastoral legacy, and we can draw from it that our own ongoing discovery of truth and meaning occurs naturally as we seek to embody soulfully our greatest ideals in our praxis of intimacy, community, and society.

Although Teresa manifested this reality in her own ways and in a very different historical context, she witnesses to the possibility of doing so in whatever circumstances one finds oneself. Further, she invites us into a community of people of spirit and heart, unbounded by space and time, a sacred circle in which we come to know and follow our hearts, support one another as we learn and speak our deepest, integrated truths, and participate in the redemptive challenges and joys of transformation.

For Further Reading

Primary Sources

María de San José Salazar. *Book for the Hour of Recreation.* Introduction and notes by Alison Weber. Translated by Amanda Powell. Chicago: University of Chicago Press, 2002.

Teresa de Jesús. *The Collected Works of St. Teresa of Avila.* Translated and introduced by Kieran Kavanaugh and Otilio Rodríguez. 3 vols. Washington, DC: Institute of Carmelite Studies, 1980–87.

———. *The Interior Castle.* Translated by Kieran Kavanaugh and Otilio Rodríguez. Mahwah, NJ: Paulist Press, 1979.

———. *Obras completas.* Edited by Enrique Llamas Martínez, Teófanes Egido, Daniel de Pablo Maroto, José Vicente Rodríguez, Fortunato Antolín, and Luis Rodríguez Martínez, under the direction of Alberto Barrientos. Madrid: Editorial de Espiritualidad, 1984.

Concordances

San José, Luis de. *Concordancias de las obras y escritos de Santa Teresa de Jesús.* Burgos: El Monte Carmelo, 1982.

Historical Studies of Teresa or Her Context

Ahlgren, Gillian T. W. *Teresa of Avila and the Politics of Sanctity.* Ithaca, NY: Cornell University Press, 1996.

Bilinkoff, Jodi. *The Avila of Saint Teresa: Religious Reform in a*

Sixteenth-Century City. Ithaca, NY: Cornell University Press, 1989.

Egido Martínez, Teófanes. "The Historical Setting of St. Teresa's Life." Translated by Steven Payne and Michael Dodd. *Carmelite Studies* 1(1980): 122–82.

Elliott, J. H. *Imperial Spain 1469-1716.* London: Pelican, 1963.

Giles, Mary E., ed., *Women in the Inquisition: Spain and the New World.* Baltimore: Johns Hopkins University Press, 1999.

Hamilton, Alastair. *Heresy and Mysticism in Sixteenth Century Spain: The Alumbrados.* Toronto: University of Toronto Press, 1992.

Madre de Dios, Efrén de la and Otger Steggink. *Tiempo y vida de Santa Teresa.* Madrid: Biblioteca de Autores Cristianos, 1968, 1977.

Perry, Mary Elizabeth. *Gender and Disorder in Early Modern Seville.* Princeton, NJ: Princeton University Press, 1990.

Weber, Alison. "Teresa's Problematic Patrons." *Journal of Medieval and Early Modern Studies* 29, no. 2 (1999): 357–79.

Literary Studies of Teresa

Barrientos, Alberto, et al. *Introducción a la lectura de Santa Teresa.* Madrid: Editorial de Espiritualidad, 1978.

García de la Concha, Victor. *El arte literario de Santa Teresa.* Barcelona: Ariel, 1978.

Rossi, Rosa. *Teresa de Avila: Biografía de una escritora.* Translated by Marieta Gargatagli. Barcelona: ICARIA, 1984.

Slade, Carole. *St. Teresa of Avila: Author of a Heroic Life.* Berkeley, CA: University of California Press, 1995.

Weber, Alison. *Teresa of Avila and the Rhetoric of Femininity.* Princeton, NJ: Princeton University Press, 1990.

Theological Studies of Teresa

Ahlgren, Gillian T. W. "Teresa of Avila, Theologian." In *Reformation Theologians,* edited by Carter Lindberg. Oxford: Basil Blackwell, 2001.

Alvarez, Tomás. *Guía al interior del Castillo: Lectura espiritual de las "Moradas."* Burgos: Editorial Monte Carmelo, 2000.

Frohlich, Mary. *The Intersubjectivity of the Mystic: A Study of Teresa of Avila's* Interior Castle. Atlanta, GA: Scholars Press, 1993.

Galilea, Segundo. *The Future of Our Past: The Spanish Mystics Speak to Contemporary Spirituality.* South Bend, IN: Ave Maria Press, 1985.

Herraiz García, Maximiliano. *Solo Dios basta: Claves de la espiritualidad Teresiana.* Madrid: Editorial de Espiritualidad, 1982.

Howells, Edward. *John of the Cross and Teresa of Avila: Mystical Knowing and Selfhood.* New York: Crossroad, 2002.

Luti, J. Mary. *Teresa of Avila's Way.* Collegeville, MN: Liturgical Press, 1991.

Trueman Dicken, E. W. *The Crucible of Love: A Study of the Mysticism of St. Teresa of Jesus and St. John of the Cross.* New York: Sheed & Ward, 1963.

Williams, Rowan. *Teresa of Avila.* Harrisburg, PA: Morehouse, 1991.

Other Biographies

Gross, Francis L., and Toni Perior Gross. *The Making of a Mystic: Seasons in the Life of Teresa of Avila.* Albany, NY: SUNY Press, 1993.

Medwick, Cathleen. *Teresa of Avila: The Progress of a Soul.* New York: Alfred A. Knopf, 1999.

Peers, E. Alison. *Mother of Carmel: A Portrait of St. Teresa of Jesus.* London: SCM Press, 1946.

Other General Works on Christian Mysticism

De Certeau, Michel. *The Mystic Fable: The Sixteenth and Seventeenth Centuries.* Chicago: University of Chicago Press, 1992.

McGinn, Bernard. *The Presence of God: A History of Western Christian Mysticism.* Vol. 1, *The Foundations of Mysticism: Origins to the Fifth Century;* Vol. 2, *The Growth of Mysticism: Gregory the Great through the Twelfth Century;* Vol. 3, *The Flowering of Mysticism:*

Men and Women in the New Mysticism—1200-1350. New York: Crossroad, 1992, 1994, 1998.

McIntosh, Mark. *Mystical Theology: The Integrity of Spirituality and Theology.* Oxford: Basil Blackwell, 1998.

A Teresian Chronology

March 28, 1515	Teresa born
Spring 1531	Enters Santa María de la Gracia, Augustinian convent, as a student in their boarding school (*Life* chap. 2)
Fall 1532	Leaves Santa María de la Gracia due to illness
November 2, 1535	Enters Carmelite Convent of the Encarnación
November 3, 1537	Makes religious profession
Fall 1538	Leaves convent due to illness; reads Francisco de Osuna's *Third Spiritual Alphabet;* illnesses continue through 1542; Teresa resides alternately with uncle, sister and father, returning to convent in 1539
December 26, 1543	Death of her father. Teresa handles legal problems surrounding his estate for many years afterward.
1554?	Scholars' general consensus as to the date of her "conversion" before the statue of Christ at the pillar; see *Life* chap. 9
1557	Consults with Francisco de Borja, S.J.
August 17, 1559	Appearance of Valdés Index of Prohibited Books; for Teresa's response, see *Life* 26:5 Autos de fe in Valladolid, Seville target *luteranos, judaizantes, moriscos;* increased inquisitional activity

1560	Consults with Pedro de Alcántara
February 7, 1562	Date of Pope Pius IV's formal permission to found the convent of San José in Avila; Teresa is traveling and receives it in July
June 1562	Finishes first redaction of *Life*
August 24, 1562	Official foundation of San José; Teresa is called back to the Encarnación almost immediately and must defend her new foundation before a town council meeting.
January 1563	Named prioress of San José; drafts the Constitutions of the Discalced Carmelite order
1564–	Promulgation of the Decrees of the Council of Trent (1545–1563), including claustration of religious women
Spring 1565?	Finishes second redaction of *Life*
1565/1566	Finishes first redaction of *Camino de perfección*
February 18, 1567	Meets with Minister General of the Carmelite order, Juan Bautista Rubeo, who authorizes her to found more convents in April 1567
August 15, 1567	Foundation of the convent in Medina del Campo
April 11, 1568	Foundation of the convent in Malagón
August 15, 1568	Foundation of convent in Valladolid
September 12, 1568	Correspondence with Juan de Avila about the orthodoxy of her mystical experiences and whether or not it was appropriate for her *Life* to circulate
November 28, 1568	Foundation of first Discalced monastery for friars in Duruelo, where John of the Cross enters
May 14, 1569	Foundation of convent in Toledo
June 28, 1569	Foundation of convent for nuns in Pastrana

July 13, 1569	Foundation of monastery for friars in Pastrana
1570	First encounter with the Inquisition; Hernando del Castillo turns the *Life* in to the Inquisitor General
November 1, 1570	Foundation of convent in Salamanca
January 25, 1571	Foundation of convent in Alba de Tormes
October 6, 1571	Elected prioress of the Encarnación; serves as prioress three years
March 19, 1574	Foundation of convent in Segovia; moves nuns from Pastrana to Segovia
December 3, 1574	Inquisitional Tribunal of Córdoba investigates the *Life* as a book of "visions and revelations"
February 24, 1575	Foundation of convent in Beas
February/March 1575	Inquisitional Tribunal of Valladolid assigns Domingo Báñez to review the *Life* for orthodoxy
May 29, 1575	Foundation of convent in Seville
January 1, 1576	Foundation of convent in Caravaca by Ana de San Alberto (acting for Teresa); Teresa is embroiled in inquisitorial investigation in Seville at this point
February 1576	Inquisitional representatives from the Tribunal of Seville interview Teresa
June-November 1577	Writes *The Interior Castle*
February 21, 1580	Foundation of convent at Villanueva de la Jara
December 29, 1580	Foundation of convent in Palencia
June 3, 1581	Foundation of convent in Soria
January 20, 1582	Foundation of convent in Granada by Ana de Jesus
April 19, 1582	Foundation of convent in Burgos
October 4, 1582	Dies in Alba de Tormes

Notes

Introduction

1. Bernard McGinn, *The Foundations of Mysticism*, vol. 1 of *The Presence of God: A History of Western Christian Mysticism* (New York: Crossroad, 1991), xiii–xiv. Earlier, McGinn cites a passage from Teresa's *Life* in which she identifies her experience of "a consciousness of the presence of God" with "mystical theology." According to McGinn, "Mystical theology is not some form of epiphenomenon, a shell or covering that can be peeled off to reveal the 'real' thing. The interactions between conscious acts and their symbolic and theoretical thematizations are much more complex than that, as the following volumes will try to show. Rather than being something added on to mystical experience, mystical theory in most cases precedes and guides the mystic's whole way of life" (ibid., xiv).

2. See Alonso Cortes, "Pleitos de los Cepeda," *Boletín de la Real Academia Española* 25 (1946): 85–110.

3. Nearly all of Teresa's brothers ended up, like many *conversos*, making careers for themselves in the New World. Teresa's older brother Hernando de Cepeda (b. 1510) went to America about 1530, where he fought in Peru during the 1530s. Rodrigo de Cepeda (b. 1511) went to America on the expedition of Pedro de Mendoza in 1535 and later died in battle. Lorenzo de Cepeda (1519–1580), whose success in Peru was greatly responsible for Teresa's foundation in Seville, spent much of his life, from 1540 to 1575, in the New World. Antonio de Cepeda (1520–1546) became a soldier in 1544 and was killed in a battle near Quito. Pedro de Cepeda (b. 1521) went to the New World in the 1540s and returned to Spain with Lorenzo in 1575. Jerónimo de Cepeda (1522–1575) went with brother Lorenzo to America, and was going to return to Spain in 1575, but died before embarking on the return trip. Agustín de Cepeda (1527–1591) was made governor of Los Quijos (Chile) in 1579, then later of Tucumán.

4. *Conversos* made possible most of Teresa's earliest foundations and, over the course of her lifetime, nine of her Discalced Carmelite convents. See

141

Alison Weber, "Teresa's Problematic Patrons," *Journal of Medieval and Early Modern Studies* 29, no. 2 (1999): 357–79.

5. In 1555 she worked with the Jesuit Juan de Pradanos, and in 1556 she took Baltasar Alvarez, S.J., as her confessor. She also consulted with Francis Borgia, who passed through Avila in 1557. For Teresa's account of this time period, see *Life,* chaps. 23 and 24.

6. A list of these theologians and pastors is contained in the brief account of her spiritual life, which she submitted to the Inquisitional Tribunal of Seville in January/February of 1576 as part of her inquisitorial investigation. See *The Collected Works of St. Teresa of Avila,* trans. Kieran Kavanaugh and Otilio Rodríguez (Washington, DC: Institute of Carmelite Studies, 1987), 1:418–25, esp. 418–22.

7. Teresa's reflections on the Index are contained in *Life* chap. 26. For commentary on its influence on Teresa, see Gillian T. W. Ahlgren, *Teresa of Avila and the Politics of Sanctity* (Ithaca, NY: Cornell University Press, 1996), 39–41.

8. For an assessment of Catholic "literacy" in Tridentine Spain, see Sara T. Nalle, *God in La Mancha: Religious Reform and the People of Cuenca, 1500–1650* (Baltimore, MD: Johns Hopkins University Press, 1992).

9. Her *Life,* for example, was reviewed by her confessor Domingo Bañez, as a formal inquisitorial censor, and was held by the Inquisitional Tribunal until 1586. For a copy of his comments, see Carole Slade, *St. Teresa of Avila: Author of a Heroic Life* (Berkeley: University of California Press, 1995), 145–48, and her reflections, 22–23. See also Ahlgren, *Teresa of Avila and the Politics of Sanctity,* 49–51.

10. For a review of the theological positions taken by readers of *The Complete Works* and the posthumous inquisitional review process they spawned, see Ahlgren, *Teresa of Avila and the Politics of Sanctity,* 114–44.

11. The letter Luis de León wrote in 1586 to Ana de Jesús, prioress of the Discalced Carmelite convent in Madrid was reprinted at the beginning of the text of Teresa's *Complete Works.* For a copy of his comments, see Luis de León, *Obras completas castellanas,* prologue and notes by Félix García (Madrid: Biblioteca de Autores Cristianos, 1959), 904–14.

12. Thus María del Nacimiento, who described "such great beauty in her face" when she wrote. See *Biblioteca mística carmelitana,* ed. Silverio de Santa Teresa, 35 vols. (Burgos: El Monte Carmelo, 1934–49), 18:315.

13. As Carole Slade notes: "The dove...became [a] standard element in the iconography of Teresa because, the brief for her canonization declares, with circular causality, the fact that 'she has been and shall be painted with a dove over her head' signifies that the doctrine in her books was 'not acquired or taught by human industry but infused by God'" (*St. Teresa of Avila: Author of a Heroic Life,* 2).

14. Alison Weber, *Teresa of Avila and the Rhetoric of Femininity* (Princeton, NJ: Princeton University Press, 1990), 11, 15; cf. Victor García de la Concha, *El arte literario de Santa Teresa* (Barcelona: Ariel, 1978).

15. See Ahlgren, *Teresa of Avila and the Politics of Sanctity,* 67–84, esp. conclusions, 83–84.

16. Rowan Williams, *Teresa of Avila* (Harrisburg, PA: Morehouse, 1991), ix. This study provides a solid general introduction to Teresa of Avila as a theologian. See also Gillian T. W. Ahlgren, "Teresa of Avila, Theologian" in *Reformation Theologians,* ed. Carter Lindberg (Oxford: Basil Blackwell, 2001), 311–24.

17. For a discussion of this tension, see Ahlgren, *Teresa of Avila and the Politics of Sanctity,* 67–84.

18. Edward Howells, *John of the Cross and Teresa of Avila: Mystical Knowing and Selfhood* (New York: Crossroad, 2002).

19. Antonio Márquez, *Literatura e Inquisición en Espana (1478–1834)* (Madrid: Taurus, 1980), 223, cited in Slade, *St. Teresa of Avila: Author of a Heroic Life,* 3.

20. See Slade, *St. Teresa of Avila: Author of a Heroic Life,* 9.

21. For a history of the Inquisition and its activities, see Henry Kamen, *Inquisition and Society in Spain in the Sixteenth and Seventeenth Centuries* (Bloomington: Indiana University Press, 1985). Important insights into the operation of the Inquisition as they relate to considerations of gender are explored in *Women in the Inquisition,* ed. Mary E. Giles (Baltimore: Johns Hopkins University Press, 1998); and Mary Elizabeth Perry, *Gender and Disorder in Early Modern Seville* (Princeton, NJ: Princeton University Press, 1990).

22. We still await a definitive English-language history of *alumbradismo;* however, an excellent Spanish-language study of the early *alumbrados* is Antonio Márquez, *Los alumbrados: Orígenes y filosofía, 1525–1559* (Madrid: Taurus, 1980). Márquez's observations are not universally applicable, however, to the second and third waves of *alumbradismo.*

23. For studies of women in similar circumstances, see the articles on Francisca Hernández, María de Cazalla, Francisca de los Apóstoles, and Ana Domenge in *Women in the Inquisition,* ed. Giles.

24. For a review and analysis of these events, see Jodi Bilinkoff, *The Avila of Saint Teresa: Religious Reform in a Sixteenth-Century City* (Ithaca, NY: Cornell University Press, 1989), 137–51.

25. For a summary of these problems, see Ahlgren, *Teresa of Avila and the Politics of Sanctity,* 47–64.

26. See "Censura del P. Bánez," in Teresa, *Obras completas,* ed. Alberto Barrientos (Madrid: Editorial de Espiritualidad, 1984), 306, 308.

27. For a summary of their content, see Ahlgren, *Teresa of Avila and the*

Politics of Sanctity, 57–58, or for a more thorough review, see Tomás Alvarez, "Esta monja: Carisma y obediencia en una relación de la Santa," *El Monte Carmelo* 78 (1970): 143–62.

28. Jerónimo Gracián, *Anotaciones al P. Ribera* in Antonio de San Joaquín, *Año teresiano, diario histórico, panegyrico moral, en que se descubren las virtudes, sucesos y maravillas de la seráphica y mystica Doctora de la Iglesia Santa Teresa de Jesús,* 12 vols. (Madrid, 1733-69), 7:149.

29. As an example of Teresa's rejection of contemporary suspicion of mental prayer and her deliberate choice to defend the legitimacy of specific religious experiences, I cite a classic passage from the *Interior Castle* in which Teresa criticized the view that visions should have no corporeal dimension that so characterized inquisitional determinations of *alumbradismo.* Reflecting on how the soul should continually meditate on the humanity of Christ, she writes: "It will also seem to you that anyone who enjoys such lofty thing will no longer meditate on the mysteries of the most sacred humanity of our Lord Jesus Christ....This is a matter I wrote about at length elsewhere [i.e., in chap. 22 of the *Life*]. They have contradicted me about it and said that I don't understand...that when souls have already passed beyond the beginning stages it is better for them to deal with things concerning the divinity and flee from corporeal things. Nonetheless, they will not make me admit that such a road is a good one....[A]lthough I've spoken on this topic at other times, I will speak of it again here that you will proceed very carefully in this matter. And take notice that I dare say you should not believe anyone who tells you something else" (*Interior Castle* VI:7:5). I will take up the role of the incarnation in the ontological transformation of the human person in discussions of the sixth dwelling places.

30. See Howells, *John of the Cross and Teresa of Avila,* 94; see also discussion below, pp. 98–105.

31. With respect to the word *consciousness,* I am referring to the definition of mysticism proposed by Bernard McGinn at the outset of his history of western Christian mysticism: "[T]he mystical element in Christianity is that part of its belief and practices that concerns the preparation for, the consciousness of, and the reaction to what can be described as the immediate or direct presence of God" (*The Foundations of Mysticism: Origins to the Fifth Century* [New York: Crossroad, 1991], xvii). Without engaging in a lengthy explanation of what he means by "consciousness," McGinn suggests that mystical consciousness is qualitatively different from ordinary realms of human consciousness: "When I speak of mysticism as involving an immediate consciousness of the presence of God I am trying to highlight a central claim that appears in almost all mystical texts. Mystics continue to affirm that their mode of access to God is radically different from that found in ordinary consciousness, even from the awareness of God gained through the usual reli-

gious activities of prayer, sacraments, and other rituals....What differentiates it from other forms of religious consciousness is its presentation as both subjectively and objectively more direct, even at times as immediate. This experience is presented as subjectively different insofar as it is affirmed as taking place on a level of the personality deeper and more fundamental than that objectifiable through the usual conscious activities of sensing, knowing, and loving. There is also an objective difference to the extent that this mode of the divine presence is said to be given in a direct or immediate way, without the usual internal and external mediations found in other types of consciousness" (ibid., xix).

32. See Mark McIntosh, *Mystical Theology: The Integrity of Spirituality and Theology* (Malden, MA: Blackwell, 1998), 4: "In the time of Edith Stein and perhaps since that time the usual definitions of spirituality and theology as separated disciplines seem less persuasive. This may be, therefore, an appropriate moment for questioning the status quo of their divorce." See also ibid.: "Perhaps today the grounds upon which spirituality and theology were clinically isolated from each other no longer exist. It was doubtful whether we could ever afford to maintain such a division in any case. The question now is whether we may find...the pattern for the re-weaving of spirituality and theology."

33. See Howells, *John of the Cross and Teresa of Avila*, 70–118.

34. Thus, theological commentary focuses almost exclusively on the second version of the *Showings*, and the first version was suppressed in most modern editions of the *Showings*. The notable exception is that of Edmund Colledge and James Walsh prepared for Paulist's Classics of Western Spirituality series. For a discussion of the evolution of Julian's theological thought, see "Introduction" in Julian of Norwich, *Showings*, ed. Edmund Colledge and James Walsh (Mahwah, NJ: Paulist Press, 1978), 17–119. Although I cannot undertake a full-blown comparison of the two figures in this book, I will refer briefly to Julian's thought when we reach the sixth dwelling places of Teresa's *Interior Castle*, because the two women appear to be engaged in a similar theological project. In asserting this, I do not mean to suggest that Julian served as a source for Teresa—directly or indirectly, that would be highly unlikely. However, both women explore how revelation enables the human person to explore in human experience the union of humanity and divinity fully realized in Christ. Both women are committed to experiencing and teaching such a process and committing it to writing. Both women write two separate treatises that reflect their ongoing theological and spiritual development—and both women's writings demonstrate clearly that their mystical knowledge of Christ led them incrementally to insights into trinitarian theology and theological anthropology—and to a resultant insistence on the continuity of humanity and divinity.

35. Thus *Life* 40:10: "Let us say, to make the comparison, that the divinity is like a very clear diamond, much greater than all the world; or like a mirror, as I said referring to the soul in that other vision, except that it is a mirror in so sublime a way that I wouldn't know how to exaggerate this. And we could say that everything we do is visible in this diamond since it is of such a kind that it contains all things within itself; there is nothing that escapes its magnitude." Earlier, Teresa had related a vision in which "my soul became recollected; and it seemed to me to be like a brightly polished mirror, without any part on the back or sides or top or bottom that wasn't totally clear. In its center Christ, our Lord, was shown to me, in the way I usually see Him. It seemed to me that I saw Him clearly in every part of my soul, as though in a mirror. And this mirror also—I don't know how to explain it—was completely engraved upon the Lord Himself by means of a very loving communication I wouldn't know how to describe" (*Life* 40:5).

36. For studies of the *Interior Castle*, see Weber, *Teresa of Avila and the Rhetoric of Femininity*, 98–122; Williams, *Teresa of Avila*, 108–42; and Howells, *John of the Cross and Teresa of Avila*, 93–118; chap. 6 of Howells's work is dedicated to reflection on the *Interior Castle*. Howells's insights, coupled with those of Mark McIntosh, indicate that we should anticipate many new and fertile discussions of the interplay of self-definition, mystical knowing, and intersubjectivity.

The First Dwelling Places

1. I have chosen the word *itinerary* here deliberately, even though it is potentially awkward, in order to recall intuitively some of the book's structural and generic parallels with Bonaventure's *Soul's Journey into God*, which also contains seven sections/stages, significant material on rapture, and a similar theological project: the careful attempt to account for the gradual resolution of the human/divine distinction through contemplation of God in and through all creation, in and through Christ, and in and through God. See Bonaventure, *Soul's Journey into God*, in *Bonaventure*, ed. and trans. Ewert Cousins, Classics of Western Spirituality (Mahwah, NJ: Paulist Press, 1979).

2. Thus, Edward Howells asserts, "The beginner starts with the image of God on the basis of faith, and not only is faith required, but Teresa says that it must be a *living* faith in order to gain what she calls self-knowledge." Further, as he notes, this faith is put into practice through the discipline of prayer: "This [self-knowledge] is acquired by the *active* practice of prayer, rather than by simple assent to the proposition that the soul is created in the image of God." See Howells, *John of the Cross and Teresa of Avila: Mystical Knowing and Selfhood* (New York: Crossroad, 2002), 97.

3. The Spanish word *moradas* has been alternately translated as "man-

sions" or "dwelling places," and there are beneficial connotations in either direction. "Mansions" readily conveys the scriptural reference described below as well as the spatious expanse of the soul. But I have chosen to use "dwelling places" throughout this text, in order to emphasize the need for the human person to dwell in each stage of the seven realms of the soul until it assimilates fully the transformative lessons of that stage. Further, I retain it in the plural as Teresa uses the word *moradas* in Spanish, to emphasize the complexity of each level of growth.

4. Recall the image of Teresa and her sisters bouncing about over dusty roads as they made their way to new foundations throughout Spain. For a review of some of the anecdotes contained in Teresa's *Book of the Foundations*, see Alison Weber, *Teresa of Avila and the Rhetoric of Femininity* (Princeton, NJ: Princeton University Press, 1990), 125–34; and for spiritual reflection on Teresa as a journeyer, see Francis L. Gross, Jr., with Toni Perior Gross, *The Making of a Mystic: Seasons in the Life of Teresa of Avila* (Albany, NY: SUNY Press, 1993), 166–69.

5. Unless otherwise identified, parenthetical references in the text throughout this book are to *Interior Castle.*

6. The metaphor of dwelling has received considerable recent attention in spiritual and theological literature. See, e.g., Lucinda A. Stark Huffaker, *Creative Dwelling: Empathy and Clarity in God and Self,* American Academy of Religion Series 98 (Atlanta, GA: Scholars Press, 1998).

7. See Howells, *John of the Cross and Teresa of Avila,* 98: "The first dwelling place is concerned with wrenching the soul away from its 'absorption' in the world as it first enters into an active relationship with God. Teresa sees this activity in terms of 'walking through' the soul, instigating movement where before there was stagnation." Howells's correlation of "walking" and "movement" within the soul is a brilliant insight; it is the metaphorical underpinning of the soul's "awakening" into the dynamic nature of God.

8. Teresa, *Interior Castle* I:1:8: "All our attention is taken up with the plainness of the diamond's setting or the outer wall of the castle; that is, with these bodies of ours."

9. The passage continues: "That person says that in her opinion if this were understood it would be impossible to sin, even though a soul would have to undergo the greatest trials imaginable in order to flee the occasions."

The Second Dwelling Places

1. In *Interior Castle* II:1:2 Teresa identifies these "poisonous beasts" as "our pastimes, business affairs, pleasures, and worldly buying and selling." They suggest "clutter" and impediments to our mindfulness. See, too, II:1:8: "Let us strive to do what lies in our power and guard ourselves against these poiso-

nous little reptiles, for the Lord often desires that dryness and bad thoughts afflict and pursue us without our being able to get rid of them."

2. Cf. *Life* 7:20-21: "I would counsel those who practice prayer to seek, at least in the beginning, friendship and association with other persons having the same interest. This is something most important even though the association may be only to help one another with prayers. The more of these prayers there are, the greater gain....Since this spiritual friendship is so extremely important for souls not yet fortified in virtue...I don't know how to urge it enough."

3. Such a community need not, of course, be one of vowed religious. But because Teresa's own context was a reformed monastic order dedicated to contemplation, the *Interior Castle* provides little insight into other forms of support for those who explore the mystical life.

The Third Dwelling Places

1. In Spanish the word *disponer,* "to dispose oneself" or "to prepare oneself," is most appropriate to use here. However, if in English self-disposal connotes a discarding of the self, this word leads us in the wrong direction. As I shall argue, it is the soul's willingness to open itself to shared identity, not the soul's total abnegation of the self, that is the primary work of these dwelling places. We are certainly speaking of the disposition of the will and quite possibly also of the "unpositioning" or relocation of one's selfhood.

2. See Matthew 19:24: "Again I tell you, it is easier for a camel to go through the eye of a needle than for a rich man to enter the kingdom of God."

3. See Teresa, *Interior Castle* IV:1:1, where she indicates, "Supernatural experiences begin here."

4. Teresa's reference to this text is explicit. Although she does not cite it, she comments, "From the time I began to speak of these dwelling places I have had this young man in mind" (*Interior Castle* III:1:6).

5. See Matthew 19:22: "When the young man heard this he went away sorrowful; for he had great possessions."

6. My translation. The metaphor of the soul as garden and the four ways of watering it are contained in *Life* chaps. 11 through 21.

7. Catherine LaCugna's description of "personhood," developed within the context of the doctrine of the Trinity provides helpful language here. She writes: "Personhood emerges in the balance between individuation and relationality, between self-possession and being possessed, that is, in interdependence. Autonomy literally means naming oneself with reference to oneself; heteronomy means naming oneself with reference to another....The doctrine of the Trinity helps us see that the true person is neither autonomous nor heteronomous but *theonomous*: The human person is named with reference to its

origin and destiny in God" (Catherine Mowry LaCugna, *God for Us: The Trinity and Christian Life* [New York: Harper Collins, 1991], 290).

8. The story of the rich young man is also critical in the narrative construction of the conversion of the desert dweller Antony the Great; see Athanasius, *The Life of Antony,* trans. Robert C. Gregg (New York: Paulist Press, 1980), 31. It is repeated in Augustine's classic account of his conversion in the *Confessions.* See Augustine, *Confessions* 8.6.

9. Cf. 1 Corinthians 13:4–8a: "Love is patient; love is kind. Love is not jealous, it does not put on airs. It is not snobbish. Love is never rude, it is not self-seeking, it is not prone to anger; neither does it brood over injuries. Love does not rejoice in what is wrong but rejoices with the truth. There is no limit to love's forbearance, to its trust, its hope, its power to endure. Love never fails."

10. The freedom and generosity of love Teresa encouraged in *Interior Castle* III:2:3–6 bear a comparison with Bernard of Clairvaux's definition of love in *On Loving God* VII:17: "God is not loved without a reward, although God should be loved without regard for one. True charity cannot be worthless, still, as 'it does not seek its own advantage,' it cannot be termed mercenary. Love pertains to the will, it is not a transaction; it cannot acquire or be acquired by a pact. Moving us freely, it makes us spontaneous. True love is content with itself; it has its reward, the object of its love." See Bernard of Clairvaux, *On Loving God* in *Treatises II: The Book on Loving God and The Steps of Humility and Pride,* trans. Robert Walton (Kalamazoo, MI: Cistercian Publications, 1980), 110.

The Fourth Dwelling Places

1. For a consideration of many sociohistorical and theological aspects of the early Christian ascetical tradition, see Peter Brown, *The Body and Society: Men, Women and Sexual Renunciation in Early Christianity* (New York: Columbia University Press, 1988); Margaret Miles, *Carnal Knowing: Female Nakedness and Religious Meaning in the Christian West* (New York: Oxford University Press, 1991); and *Asceticism,* ed. Vincent L. Wimbush and Richard Valentasis (New York: Oxford University Press, 1995).

2. In articulating a new spiritual vocabulary Michael Downey makes a similar point (*Altogether Gift: A Trinitarian Spirituality* [Maryknoll, NY: Orbis Books, 2000], 111): "Christian *ascesis* has all too often been understood narrowly as mortification of the flesh, and has not been applied consistently to other demanding aspects of the Christian life such as the rigorous sacrifices entailed in marital and family life, especially caring for one's children; the uncertainties of agrarian life; the daily struggles for mere subsistence; complex decisions about the use and disposition of goods; the chaste exercise of sexuality for non-celibates; responsibility for the earth; the discipline required

for education and study; proper care and exercise of the body including nutrition, diet, balance of leisure and work; and the tedium of too much work. These dimensions of Christian life were rarely addressed in treatments of the rigors of asceticism. Yet this is the very 'stuff' of Christian living—from font, to table, to cross."

3. Teresa, *Interior Castle* IV:1:12: "So, Lord, bring us to the place where these miseries will not taunt us, for they seem sometimes to be making fun of the soul. Even in this life, the Lord frees the soul from these miseries when it reaches the last dwelling place, as we shall say later if God wills."

4. See Bernard of Clairvaux, *On Loving God,* ed. Robert Walton, in *Treatises II: The Steps of Humility and Pride and On Loving God* (Kalamazoo, MI: Cistercian Publications, 1973), 118–19.

5. For Bernard these raptures are experienced in the fourth stage of loving God; for Teresa, they are located in the sixth dwelling places.

6. For Edward Howells, Teresa's reflection on the different natures of the two fountains is not only a reflection of the difference between natural and supernatural prayer but also a reflection of a deep dichotomy between human nature and God. Commenting on the images, he states, "Teresa draws attention to the discontinuity between these two sources of prayer with greater clarity than in previous works." And he notes, "This strong distinction between the mediated and unmediated sources of the two kinds of prayer is carried through to Teresa's distinction between 'two troughs': not only are there two founts, but they flow into distinct parts of the soul or troughs" (*John of the Cross and Teresa of Avila: Mystical Knowing and Selfhood* [New York: Crossroad, 2002], 102). This indicates, for Howell, the introduction of a division of the soul into an interior and an exterior part, a division he reflects on more fully in his commentary on the sixth dwelling places. See his discussion of the expansion of the soul (ibid., 103–5); see also pp. 78–80, where he introduces the problem of the division of the soul. I am not sure that Teresa is postulating an inherent division in the soul but rather working as well as she can, linguistically, to express the soul's limited self-knowledge at this stage. Certainly, at this level of development, the soul has not yet entered into a capacity to know, experientially, its own nature, especially to know its own essential unity. Whatever it posits about itself will be based on this still limited self-knowledge. Insofar as it experiences itself as divided—or, perhaps better, *partial*—its self-representation and all of the subsequent metaphors used to describe itself will reinforce that stage of self-knowledge. Certainly, the insights it experiences in moments of spiritual delight reveal to the soul both its own limited capacity in and of itself and its deeper and wider possibilities in partnership with God.

7. Cf. Augustine, *Confessions* 10.27.

8. For another discussion of the "center of the soul" see Howells, *John of*

the Cross and Teresa of Avila, 114–18. Here Howells examines stages in the development of Teresa's understanding of the "center" from the first through the seventh dwelling places, noting how "expansion" of this center is related to the soul's expanded self-knowledge. However, there is no analysis of how the fourth dwelling places fit into this expansion. See p. 115. Howells has already argued, however, that "[t]he first apprehension of true self-knowledge, which is the first knowledge of the relationship between the soul and God, is thus shown to be an imperfect yet real preview of mystical knowing, possessing something of the same mutual dynamism between the soul and God. Even though the preparatory stages cannot *anticipate* that mutual dynamism of union, an underlying pattern is established in the soul's activity which will be taken up in union" (p. 99).

The Fifth Dwelling Places

1. Bernard McGinn, "Foreword," in Denys Turner, *Eros and Allegory: Medieval Exegesis of the Song of Songs* (Kalamazoo, MI: Cistercian Publications, 1995), 13.

2. Turner, *Eros and Allegory,* 25.

3. Haunani-Kay Trask, *Eros and Power: The Promise of Feminist Theory* (Philadelphia: University of Pennsylvania Press, 1986), 92.

4. Rita Nakashima Brock, *Journeys by Heart: A Christology of Erotic Power* (New York: Crossroad, 1988), 40; see 25–49 for a deeper discussion of the nature of *eros* and erotic power.

5. Turner, *Eros and Allegory,* 49 (emphasis his).

6. For a discussion of God as Eros, see Bernard McGinn, "God as Eros: Metaphysical Foundations of Christian Mysticism," in *New Perspectives on Historical Theology: Essays in Memory of John Meyendorff,* ed. Bradley Nassif (Grand Rapids: William B. Eerdmans, 1991), 189–209.

7. Turner, *Eros and Allegory,* 58.

8, Cf. Teresa, *Interior Castle* V:1:3: "There is no need here to use any technique to suspend the mind since all the faculties are asleep in this state—and truly asleep—to the things of the world and to ourselves....In sum, it is like one who in every respect has died to the world so as to live more completely in God."

9. See Catherine Mowry LaCugna, *God for Us: The Trinity and Christian Life* (New York: Harper Collins, 1991), 290; see pp. 41–42 above, and esp. p. 148 n. 7.

10. Turner, *Eros and Allegory,* 61 (emphasis his).

11. Indeed, passages in V:1:11 might seem to warrant such an interpretive approach; for example, "I understand this union to be the wine cellar where the Lord wishes to place us when He desires and as He desires. But however

great the effort we make to do so, we cannot enter. His Majesty must place us there and enter Himself into the center of our soul."

12. Thus, Teresa precedes the passage cited above with "Now I recall, in saying that we have no part to play, what you have heard the Bride say in the Song of Songs: 'He brought me into the wine cellar' (or, placed me there, I believe it says). And it doesn't say that she went. And she says also that she went looking about in every part of the city for her Beloved." Thus her scriptural commentary includes the observation that the soul actively prepares and disposes itself for relational encounter. See V:1:11.

13. Thus Howells writes: "The purpose of the true union [described in the fifth dwelling places] is to introduce a *corrective* to her old view, which left little room for the human activity of the soul in union. Teresa wishes to point out that while union introduces something 'wholly other' into the soul, it need not for that reason remove the soul from its full creaturely humanity, *provided* that its humanity is joined with Christ" (*John of the Cross and Teresa of Avila: Mystical Knowing and Selfhood* [New York: Crossroad, 2002], 107–8). The emphasis is his, but is unnecessary, as Teresa clearly states that the "death" of the caterpillar is the soul's "dying" in Christ to live again in Christ. See Teresa, *Interior Castle*, IV:2:4. Howells makes a similar point in defense of the soul's continuing agency, noting that it becomes a form of mutual agency, like that of Christ. See p. 116: "This does not imply that the soul has become an automaton with no free will of its own. On the contrary, the mutually reflective nature of this understanding permits the soul to see its actions as self-chosen even though they come immediately from God's will. In the act of understanding God's will, it also sees its own will distinctly from God's will, and acts out of the trinitarian mutuality between them, with an agency that is both human and divine."

14. Elizabeth A. Johnson, *Consider Jesus: Waves of Renewal in Christology* (New York: Crossroad, 1990), 20.

15. Ibid., 108.

16. Cf. Pierre Teilhard de Chardin, "The Mystical Milieu," cited in Harvey D. Egan, *An Anthology of Christian Mysticism* (Collegeville, MN: Liturgical Press, 1996), 581: "The mystic suffers more than others from the tendency of created things to crumble into dust: Instinctively and obstinately, he searches for the stable, the unfailing, the absolute; but so long as he remains in the domain of outward appearances, he meets with nothing but disappointment."

17. As this disintegration is accomplished, Teresa comes to see herself as a self-in-God and all living things as "being in God." See, e.g., Teresa, *Interior Castle* VI:10:2: "In this vision it is revealed how all things are seen in God and how God has them all in Godself."

18. Here, Teresa is describing her past experiences in the third person.

19. Thus Howells: "This 'division in her soul' was an accurate reflection by Teresa on the inherent conflict in her anthropology between the interior and exterior parts of the soul in union. The interior is separated from the exterior by the ontological gap between its divine life of union with God and the merely human 'trials and occupations' that beset the exterior in the world" (*John of the Cross and Teresa of Avila,* 79).

20. Teresa, *Interior Castle* V:3:7: "What do you think His will is, daughters? That we be completely perfect. See what we lack to be one with Him and His Father as His Majesty asked. I tell you I am writing this with much pain upon seeing myself so far away—and all through my own fault." This seems to be a conflation of John 17:22–23: "And the glory that you have given me, I have given to them, that they may be one, even as we are one: I in them and you in me; that they may be perfected in unity" and "In a word, you must be made perfect as your heavenly Father in heaven is perfect" (Matt 5:48).

21. Teresa, *Interior Castle* V:2:12: "Haven't you heard it said of the bride— for I have already mentioned it elsewhere here but not in this sense—that God brought her into the inner wine cellar and put charity in order within her? Well, that is what I mean." This enables a comparison of Teresa's understanding of growth in love with that of Bernard of Clairvaux; see *On Loving God* and his discussion of the ordering of charity in *Sermons on the Song of Songs.*

The Sixth Dwelling Places

1. Rowan Williams, *Teresa of Avila* (Harrisburg, PA: Morehouse, 1991), 136.

2. Edward Howells, *John of the Cross and Teresa of Avila: Mystical Knowing and Selfhood* (New York: Crossroad, 2002), 94 (emphasis his).

3. Ibid.

4. Ibid., 95. With respect to Howells's use of the term *inner-trinitarian,* Catherine Mowry La Cugna would argue that this sets up ultimately false distinctions between God's "inner life," God's ecstatic nature, and God's relationship with all that pours out of God's creativity. Indeed, as she argues, "The life of God—precisely because God is triune—does not belong to God alone. God who dwells in inaccessible light and eternal glory comes to us in the face of Christ and the activity of the Holy Spirit. Because of God's outreach to the creature, God is said to be essentially relational, ecstatic, fecund, alive as passionate love. Divine life is therefore also *our* life" (*God for Us: The Trinity and Christian Life* [New York: Harper Collins, 1991], 1 [emphasis hers]).

5. As LaCugna reminds us: "The doctrine of the Trinity is ultimately therefore a teaching not about the abstract nature of God, nor about God in isolation from everything other than God, but a teaching about God's life with us and our life with each other. Trinitarian theology could be described

as par excellence a theology of relationship, which explores the mysteries of love, relationship, personhood and communion within the framework of God's self-revelation in the person of Christ and the activity of the Spirit" (*God for Us*, 1).

6. Ibid., 284. Earlier, LaCugna asserts: "Theosis, or becoming God is the proper *telos* of the Christian person. *Theosis* is eschatological because it points toward the proper end of the human being which is perfection in the image and likeness of God. As noted before, becoming God obviously cannot mean becoming the divine *ousia*; as beings who have a beginning we cannot become the Unoriginate Origin. *Theosis* means being conformed in our personal existence to God's personal existence, achieving right relationship and genuine communion in every respect, at every level" (pp. 283–84).

7. Williams, *Teresa of Avila*, 136.

8. LaCugna, *God for Us*, 270. Her summary of the history of the term *perichōrēsis* continues: "Effective as a defense both against tritheism and Arian subordinationism, *perichoresis* expressed the idea that the three divine persons mutually inhere in one another, draw life from one another, 'are' what they are by relation to one another....No person exists by him/herself or is referred to him/herself; this would produce number and therefore division within God. Rather, to be a divine person is to be *by nature* in relation to other persons. Each divine person is irresistibly drawn to the other, taking his/her existence from the other, containing the other in him/herself, while at the same time pouring self out into the other. Cyril of Alexandria called this movement a 'reciprocal iruption.' While there is no blurring of the individuality of each person, there is also no separation. There is only the communion of love in which each person comes to be (in the sense of *hyparxeos*) what he/she is, entirely with reference to the other. Each person expresses both what he/she is (and, by implication, what the other two are), and at the same time expresses what God is: ecstatic, relational, dynamic, vital."

9. Ibid., 271.

10. Ibid.: "*Perichoresis* provides a dynamic model of persons in communion based on mutuality and interdependence. The model of *perichoresis* avoids the pitfalls of locating the divine unity either in the divine substance (Latin) or exclusively in the person of the Father (Greek), and locates unity instead in diversity, in a true *communion* of persons."

11. I will have to set to one side, for now, exploration of the very pregnant suggestion that there is an implicit link between trinitarian theology and the nature of God as *eros*. But current scholarship in both of these areas could be placed in very fruitful theological conversation, one that would surely facilitate deeper connections between the Christian mystical tradition and current constructive theology.

12. Thus, Denys Turner paraphrases the sixth-century Neoplatonic mys-

tic Pseudo-Dionysius; see Turner, *Eros and Allegory: Medieval Exegesis of the Song of Songs* (Kalamazoo, MI: Cistercian Publications, 1995), 47, 48, and the discussion on pp. 47–56. See also Bernard McGinn, "God as Eros: Metaphysical Foundations of Christian Mysticism," in *New Perspectives on Historical Theology: Essays in Memory of John Meyendorff,* ed. Bradley Nassif (Grand Rapids: William B. Eerdmans, 1991), 199–202; and idem, *The Foundations of Mysticism,* vol. 1 of *The Presence of God: A History of Western Christian Mysticism* (New York: Crossroad, 1991), 157–82.

13. Thus, for example, Pseudo-Dionysius, cited in Turner, *Eros and Allegory,* 48. His third-century predecessor, Origen, expressed a strikingly similar proposition at the outset of his *Commentary on the Song of Songs,* one that then frames his entire interpretation of the book: "I do not think one could be blamed if one called God Passionate Love (*eros/amor*), just as John calls him Charity (*agapē/caritas*)." After some discussion of the parallel use of these terms, Origen advises: "You must take whatever scripture says about charity (*caritas*) as if it had been said in reference to passionate love (*amor*), taking no notice of the difference in terms, for the same meaning is conveyed in both" (*Commentary on the Song of Songs,* trans. R. P. Lawson [Westminster, MD: Newman Press, 1957], 32–33). For a discussion of the implications of this in Origen's thought and in the Christian tradition more generally, see McGinn, *Foundations of Mysticism,* 118–26.

14. For more discussion of this problem, see McGinn, *Foundations of Christian Mysticism,* 118–19, with its corresponding notes: "The arguments of some modern psychologists that the introduction of considerable erotic language about God into a mystical account cannot be more than a disguise and an attempt at sublimating hidden sexual urges, and the claims of some philosophers that Western philosophical and theological notions of love are erotic idealizations that remove the subject from the reality of desire by making the basis for some form of mental glorification, illustrate the fundamental differences between the way traditional Christian mystics viewed love and desire and how this force is often seen in the contemporary world. The mystics insisted that they were neither disguising nor idealizing *eros,* but rather transforming it by leading it back to its original form."

15. See LaCugna, *God for Us,* 289: "The measure of what is 'natural' with respect to being human is what brings about the full realization of persons as well as the communion of persons with one another. The achievement of personhood is the fulfillment of the *telos* (proper end) of the nature."

16. Without trying to whitewash the complex and tempestuous movements of the soul in this stage—the seemingly life-threatening waves of rapture Teresa describes—I must reject absolutely what I have heard some recent commentators refer to as "Teresa's theology of rape," a perhaps provocative but certainly irresponsible reading of the text. The profound experiences of

God at this stage are thorough and, as she describes, sudden, abrupt, and outside of the soul's power to control: foreign, at first, and overwhelming. If this is a kind of violence, it is comparable to the "shattering" of the false self, the illusion of the self's independence and autonomy. I believe this is Rowan Williams's own ultimate conclusion, even though I am uncomfortable with his use of the phrase "divine violence" to describe these experiences. See Williams, *Teresa of Avila,* 140: "She assumes that we are likely to be strangers to ourselves and that we (like her beloved Augustine) need a measure of divine violence to be brought home: it is not natural to us to be natural. But this means that all the records in Teresa's work of violent and disorienting episodes are misunderstood if read simply as a characterization of something called 'mystical' experience: the question to which she is finally seeking an answer is how a self compulsively at odds with its own real good and liable to produce any number of self-justifying and self-flattering fantasies may come to *belong* in the single movement of God's love, making and affirming and renewing the concrete world of bodies in communication."

17. Turner, *Eros and Allegory,* 58. The continuation of Turner's analysis is another important rejoinder to the idea that union with God entails a "surrender" of agency. He writes: "In a parallel way the language of *eros* is the language in which the transcendence of the dichotomy between necessity and freedom is achieved. *Eros* imposes obligations more binding—and so in a sense more 'necessary'—than any which the force of moral laws could impose; and yet, within *eros,* the language of 'imposition' and 'obligation' is itself wholly inappropriate, insofar as 'imposition' and 'obligation' can only be construed in contrast with the freedom of lover and beloved. For within the 'necessities' of erotic mutuality, love and beloved exchange with one another the gift of their own freedom, so each lives within the one freedom of both. Within that freedom they make and respond to absolute demands on one another. Erotic love is necessity lived in the mode of freedom and freedom lived within the mode of necessity. Within *eros,* necessity and freedom live within each other and transform each other just as lover and beloved do" (pp. 58–59).

18. See Origen, *Commentary on the Song of Songs,* 32. Note that this reference is embedded in the fuller discussion of the interchangeable nature of *eros* and *agapē* in God, referred to above. Interestingly, later on, in the third book of his commentary, Origen comments on this same "wound" as a wound of "charity" (*agapē*) (see p. 198).

19. For reflections on medieval explorations of the potential of the body to facilitate mystical union, see Caroline Walker Bynum, *The Resurrection of the Body in Western Christianity, 200–1336* (New York: Columbia University Press, 1995); Amy Hollywood, *The Soul as Virgin Wife: Mechthild of Magde-*

burg, Marguerite Porete, and Meister Eckhart (Notre Dame, IN: University of Notre Dame Press, 1995), esp. 26–39, 44–52, 73–78, 180–93.

20. Recall that the Latin for wound, *vulnis*, forms the root for the state of being we call vulnerability. At the level of the sixth dwelling places, vulnerability is indicative of the soul's capacity to be transformed by and in unitive encounters, to have its selfhood stretch and be stretched. It is therefore a state to be cultivated, as it represents openness to deeper intersubjectivity. For a brief discussion of vulnerability as a part of relational ontology, see Rita Nakashima Brock, *Journeys by Heart: A Christology of Erotic Power* (New York: Crossroad, 1991), 7–24.

21. See Dorothee Soelle, "Outline for a Mystical Journey," in *Mysticism and Social Transformation,* ed. Janet K. Ruffing (Syracuse: Syracuse University Press, 2001), 48: "To miss God is one form of what the tradition has also termed 'to suffer God.' Becoming empty means not only to rid ourselves of superficial ballast but also to enter isolation…to praise God and to miss God as nothing else leads to a living in God, which the tradition has called the *via unitiva.*"

22. Thus Jacques Lacan, *Feminine Sexuality: Jacques Lacan and the Ecole Freudienne,* ed. Juliet Mitchell and Jacqueline Rose (New York: Pantheon Press), 147, who, as Luce Irigaray and Grace Jantzen following her rightly point out, never bothered to read Teresa's own words but took his impressions from Bernini's statue, *St. Teresa in Ecstasy.* See Grace Jantzen, *Becoming Divine: Towards a Feminist Philosophy of Religion* (Manchester: Manchester University Press, 1998), 46–53.

23. Thus Teresa, *Interior Castle* VI:4:4: "It indeed seems in accord with the deep love the soul feels that God is drawing these very depths after God."

24. Although Bernard McGinn expresses this a bit differently, he, too, is careful to locate ecstasy beyond a particular experience or set of experiences. In his analysis of the thirteenth-century mystic Hadewijch, for example, he suggests that the deepest mystical consciousness leads beyond any particular kind of ecstatic experience. Thus he writes, "Hadewijch, despite the ecstatic experiences she describes with such ardor, insists that experiences of fruition are not the goal. What is essential is the recognition of God's presence in absence, the realization of the joy that can be found in the midst of suffering, and the adherence to the faith hidden in the midst of 'unfaith'" ("Suffering, Emptiness and Annihilation in Three Beguine Mystics," in *Homo Medietas: Aufsätze zu Religiosität, Literatur und Denkformen des Menschen vom Mittelalter bis in die Neuzeit,* ed. Claudia Briner-von der Heyde and Niklaus Largier [New York: Peter Lang, 1999], 162).

25. While Teresa is clear about the damage caused to humanity by the Fall, she is equally clear, perhaps even more insistent, about the "magnificent

beauty of a soul and its marvelous capacity" (*Interior Castle* I:1:1). Her affirmation of the created goodness of humanity should override other hermeneutical concerns, even as they need to be explored.

26. While describing Origen's "mystical gnosis," and intellectual and affective "new type of knowing"—which he does not call "erotic knowing"—McGinn writes, "Origen's mysticism centers on the transformation of eros ii, the power of yearning desire implanted in the soul by the God who is EROS I ....This is a new type of knowing...a *pathein* not a *mathein*, that is, the experience of something received in the soul, not something learned by one's own efforts" (*Foundations of Mysticism*, 125). See also p. 120: "If, as Origen believed, eros has its source above and has been implanted in us by God-Eros (we could call this EROS I), the motive force powering the soul's ascent must be the transformation of the eros gone awry in us (eros ii) back to its transcendental starting place."

27. When not accompanied by a life of dedication to the mystical journey and to the theological insights it reflects, such experiences might well be called "paramystical phenomena." But in Teresa's case this term is not appropriate, as she very carefully integrates these embodied experiences into her understanding of the mystical life, adding an incarnational dimension to her theology.

28. By *chronos* I mean the dimension of time that is linear, progressive, and chronological, in which a person can trace a narrative of his or her life. This is the dimension of time that we experience most regularly and by which we often define our life experiences. By *kairos* I refer to the qualitative sense of time, a time that defines itself by and through the intensity of what is experienced. The experience of labor and childbirth, which involves a kind of suspension of chronological time and an absorption into the experience, would exemplify a "*kairos* moment" or a timeless, absorbing space, where the internal dynamics of the experience mark and shape our sense of time. The *chronos-kairos* distinction is also indicative of the ways in which historical events define our reality or the ways in which ontological processes define reality, suggested in the introduction in the comparison of the structure of the *Life* versus the structure of the *Interior Castle*.

29. Note that this second, even more impassioned search of the lover for the beloved in Song of Songs 5:6–8 culminates in the declaration that the lover is wounded with love: "I opened to my beloved, but my beloved had turned and gone. My soul failed me when he spoke. I sought him, but found him not; I called him, but he gave no answer. The watchmen found me, as they went about in the city; they beat me, they wounded me, they took away my mantle, those watchmen of the walls. I adjure you, O daughters of Jerusalem, if you find my beloved, that you tell him I am sick with love" (RSV).

30. Howells, *John of the Cross and Teresa of Avila*, 112.

31. Teresa, *Interior Castle* VI:2:4: "And since the spark was not enough to set the soul on fire, and the fire is so delightful, the soul is left with that pain; but the spark merely by touching the soul produces that effect....just as the fire is about to start, the spark goes out and the soul is left with the desire to suffer again that loving pain the spark causes."

32. While not mentioning Teresa, Karl Rahner notes the evidence of "authentic trinitarian mysticism" and lays out a means for understanding the relationship of revelation to God's self-communication that could then be applied to revelatory mystical experience. See Karl Rahner, *The Trinity*, trans. Joseph Donceel (New York: Crossroad, 1997), esp. 36–37: "Here is the absolute mystery revealed to us only by Christ: God's self-communication is truly a *self*-communication. He does not merely indirectly give his creature some share of himself by creating and giving us created and finite realities through his omnipotent *efficient* causality. In a *quasi-formal* causality he really and in the strictest sense of the word bestows *himself*. Now the testimony of revelation in Scripture tells us that this self-communication of God has a threefold aspect. It is the self-communication in which that which is given remains sovereign, incomprehensible, continuing, even as received, to dwell in its uncontrollable incomprehensible originality. It is a self-communication in which the God who manifests himself 'is there' as self-uttered truth and as freely, historically disposing sovereignty. It is a self-communication, in which the God who communicates himself causes in the one who receives him the act of loving welcome, and causes it in such a way that his welcoming does not bring the communication down to the purely created level" (emphasis his).

33. See Augustine, *On the Trinity* 8.5, to which I think many interesting parallels can be drawn. Here Augustine grapples with the role of love in forming the ontological bridge between God and humanity, specifically in the act of loving others and loving God we begin to participate in the being of the God who is love.

34. See VI:1:7; see also chapter four of the *Life*. This suggests, of course, that the soul may experience visions and rapture *before* the sixth dwelling places.

35. Howells, *John of the Cross and Teresa of Avila*, 112.

36. This is the same conclusion as that of Origen in the prologue to his *Commentary on the Song of Songs*. For example: "We must recognize, therefore, that the charity of God is always directed towards God, from whom also it takes its origin, and looks back towards the neighbour, with whom it is in kinship as being similarly created in incorruption. So you must take whatever Scripture says about charity as if it had been said with reference to passionate love, taking no notice of the difference of terms; for the same meaning is conveyed by both." Or, "So it makes no difference whether we speak of having a

passion for God, or of loving Him; and I do not think one could be blamed if one called God Passionate Love (Amorem) just as John calls him Charity (Caritatem)" (*Commentary on the Song of Songs*, 34, 35). See also discussion in Bernard McGinn, "God as Eros: Metaphysical Foundations of Christian Mysticism," in *New Perspectives on Historical Theology: Essays in Memory of John Meyendorff*, ed. Bradley Nassif (Grand Rapids: William B. Eerdmans, 1992), 189–209.

37. Recall that Bernard of Clairvaux's fourth stage of love in *On Loving God* is when "the soul loves itself for God's sake." See Bernard of Clairvaux, *On Loving God*, in *Treatises II: The Book on Loving God and The Steps of Humility and Pride*, trans. Robert Walton (Kalamazoo, MI: Cistercian Publications, 1980), 119–21.

38. Howells notes the importance of this theological turn by comparing Teresa's perspective on the incarnation in the *Interior Castle* with that of the *Life*, noting that by the time she wrote the *Interior Castle* Teresa was "clear that Christ is to be found not just in active work or in pictures used to temper the divine force of union, but in a union of human and divine which is both exterior *and* interior to the soul. This union of human and divine in Christ is the material (*cosa*) by which the soul is expanded to have the capacity for God, that is, transformed by favors into the human-and-divine form of Christ" (*John of the Cross and Teresa of Avila*, 109).

39. Ibid.

40. Thus Howells concludes, "Without this mediation of Christ, both interiorly and exteriorly, we, as human, remain ontologically separate from God and opposed to the divine influx of union" (*John of the Cross and Teresa of Avila*, 109). But if the Logos is part of God's creative activity, I am not sure that we can assert more than human ignorance of its own unitive nature (as opposed to "opposition"), the precise form of self-knowledge the soul is learning at this stage.

41. Thus Howells: "Most importantly, the form in which the soul becomes divine in its depth is to take on an explicitly *trinitarian structure* through which it participates in God by sharing in the immediate relations of the persons of the Trinity, and this leads to the intellectual vision of the Trinity in the seventh dwelling place. This trinitarian participation is seen in the increasing ability of the soul to receive and distinguish the overflowing dynamism of favors within itself and in the growing mutuality and equality of its relationship with God" (*John of the Cross and Teresa of Avila*, 112).

42. Howells, *John of the Cross and Teresa of Avila*, 113.

43. I am using "incarnational potential" to suggest that the soul, in and through Christ, shares in the union of humanity and divinity that the Christian tradition refers to as "hypostatic union." According to the Chalcedonian

formula, Christ was fully human and fully divine in unbreakable unity, in such a way that anything that can be predicated of the one nature can also be predicated of the other. See discussion above, pp. 69–71.

44. Howells, *John of the Cross and Teresa of Avila,* 113.

45. Ibid., 71, 79–80. All of these ideas are developed in a fuller discussion of Teresa's changing anthropology, pp. 70–118.

46. Edmund Colledge and James Walsh, "Introduction," in *Showings* (Mahwah, NJ: Paulist Press, 1978), 24. For Julian's reflections on the gradual resolution of human-divine perspectival differences as the soul moves into greater ontological union with God, see pp. 193–94, 198–99, 204–5, 210–13, 218–20, 230–31, 256–62, 265–82, 288–92, 306–7, 335–37. Many of these references contain her reflections on how both bodily and spiritual visions are integral to realization of the full union of humanity and divinity in Christ and in the human person.

The Seventh Dwelling Places

1. With references to the Spirit of light and truth.

2. See Luke 10:38–42 and Luke 7:37–38, to which Teresa refers in *Interior Castle* VII:4:12–13. For discussion, see pp. 118–19 below. The states of being represented by Mary and Martha may be as characteristic of the divine as of the soul; that is, the state of "Mary" may represent the unitive way of being, while the state of Martha may represent the state of coexistence. God has knowledge of Godself as essential unity at the same time that God knows God's self as distinct persons within that unity. Martha represents the separability of the persons of the Trinity and their ability, as persons, to work with humanity.

3. Teresa, *Interior Castle* VII:1:8: "If the soul does not fail God, He will never fail, in my opinion, to make His presence clearly known to it. It has strong confidence that since God has granted this favor He will not allow it to lose the favor. Though the soul thinks this, it goes about with greater care than ever not to displease Him in anything."

4. For a history of interpretation of this passage within the mystical tradition, see Bernard McGinn, "Love, Knowledge and *Unio Mystica* in the Western Christian Tradition" in Moshe Idel and Bernard McGinn, *Mystical Union and Monotheistic Faith: An Ecumenical Dialogue* (New York: Macmillan, 1989), 59–86, esp. 82, where he treats of Teresa's understanding of mystical union. In Teresa's case, it is difficult to know exactly how she understood the mechanics of this union. When commenting on the text from Paul, she originally wrote: "We are made one spirit with God if we love Him; he [i.e., Paul] doesn't say that we are joined with Him…but are made one spirit with Him." See Teresa, *Interior Castle* VII:2:5, n. 9.

5. See Galatians 2:20: "I have been crucified with Christ; it is no longer I who live, but Christ who lives in me." See also Philippians 1:21: "For me to live is Christ, and to die is gain."

6. See Teresa, *Interior Castle* VII:3:12: "I am amazed as well to see that when the soul arrives here all raptures are taken away. Only once in a while are they experienced and then without those transports and that flight of the spirit....[T]he poor little butterfly that went about so apprehensive that everything frightened it and made it fly...has found its repose, or has seen so much that nothing frightens it....[and] this great weakness is taken away... [T]he Lord has now fortified, enlarged, and made the soul capable."

7. Teresa, *Interior Castle* VII:2:6: "And that its life is Christ is understood better, with the passing of time, by the effects this life has."

Walking with Teresa Today

1. Segundo Galilea, *The Future of Our Past: The Spanish Mystics Speak to Contemporary Spirituality* (Notre Dame, IN: Ave Maria Press, 1985), 26.

2. Ibid.

3. Janet K. Ruffing, "Introduction," in *Mysticism and Social Transformation*, ed. Janet K. Ruffing (Syracuse: Syracuse University Press, 2001), 12. And of mysticism's inherent liberatory dimension, Segundo Galilea writes: "The practice of interior liberation, which is a distinctive trait of Christian spirituality, is just as important as pastoral or political practices. There is no need to recall here that the Christian idea of liberation holds that, without human beings who are free, converted from the worship of their idols and made capable of fraternity, solidarity and justice, the process of social liberation would stand in jeopardy. In this sense, the Christian mystique is essentially liberating; it liberates us so that we in turn may liberate others. It reminds us that human oppressions, and the forms of injustice and servitude that human beings impose on other human beings cannot be eliminated by purely sociopolitical, economic, educational or psychological activities" (*Future of Our Past*, 81).

4. For a brief overview of some of these issues, see Francis L. Gross and Toni Perior Gross, *The Making of a Mystic: Seasons in the Life of Teresa of Avila* (Albany, NY: SUNY Press, 1993), 143–69.

5. See, e.g., Antonio Damasio, *The Feeling of What Happens: Body and Emotion in the Making of Consciousness* (New York: Harcourt Brace, 1999).

6. Gross and Gross, *Making of a Mystic*, 202.